Misadventures

of a Zoo Keeper

2nd Edition

Misadventures

of a Zoo Keeper

2nd Edition

Bill Naylor

Published by www.lulu.co.uk

© Copyright Bill Naylor 2014

MISADVENTURES OF A ZOO KEEPER

This 2nd edition

First published by www.lulu.com 2013
2nd edition published by www.lulu.com 2014

ISBN 978-1-326-02093-4

Book formatted by www.bookformatting.co.uk.

Printed and bound in the United Kingdom.

Contents

Dedicated to Penny, Jason and Natasha.
And the memory of Mum, Dad & Charlie
With thanks to numerous individuals of other species,
who often assaulted me, but from whom I learned so much.

Illustrated by the author

MARATHON MAN

On the day I started as a trainee at Chester Zoo, the largest zoo in the UK, another young guy who was leaving told me.

"There's far too much walking in this job, I'm going back to being a postman."

Being dispatched to feed or cater for any animal could mean an hour's walk. Even longer, if the zoo was crowded with visitors. Even longer, when you were plagued with visitor's questions, some of which could render you speechless.

"Which way to the Dodos?"

"We don't have any Dodos."

"None at all?"

"Not at the moment."

"Are they hard to breed then?"

"Sort of impossible."

"So where do you suggest we go to see Dodos?"

"You could try Dodo land. "

Once while feeding the penguins, I was accosted by a young guy whose adoring girlfriend was wrapped around him, her mouth glued to his neck.

"How do you stop the penguins from flying away?"

"They can't fly," I replied.

His giggling girlfriend leaned towards me.

"There's nothing he doesn't know about wild life. He watches that David Attenburger all the time." The guy rounded on me.

"What do you mean penguins can't fly? What do you think those flippy flappy things sticking out of their sides are for ?"

"They're flippers, perfect for swimming under water, but useless for flying."

"Then tell me this know all. Where do penguins come from?"

"The south pole," I replied.

"Exactly!" he said nodding smugly at his girlfriend.

"And how do you think they got there?"

I shrugged, "Must have flown."

Feeding zoo animals appears an easy task. But it can involve hazards from the most unlikely zoo inmates. A pair of small parakeets were mysteriously christened Black and Decker. I was warned never to let them get too close when cleaning their aviary.

To me they appeared tame and friendly and amusingly did everything together. It only came to light why they had been christened Black and Decker, when they both landed on my head and proceeded to industriously drill and hammer in unison.

They were one of many species that senior keepers warned,

"Watch em, or they'll have you." Every time I commented on how tame or appealing a particular animal was, the phrase,

"They'll have you," would surface. Older keepers proudly wore scars from bites, kicks and other assaults.

A lion keeper called Stubby, would boast, "I've given twenty years to working with big cats." He'd then hold up his right hand, where two half fingers were clearly missing. "And I've got the scars to prove it." This earned him a certain kudos among his fellow keepers. Slightly more, than if he'd mentioned his accident in a previous job, operating a bread-slicing machine.

Some keepers used injuries real and imagined as an excuse to avoid work.

One keeper claimed early in his career, an orang-utan had grabbed his ears through the bars of its cage, twisting them permanently into the horizontal position.

His claim could never be verified as he always wore his hair long, extending below his ears. But he would regularly down tools when grey clouds gathered, complaining, if he worked in the rain, his ears would fill with water.

Another keeper claimed he had sustained a serious injury while training dolphins. Since then he had avoided all heavy lifting, due to what he called 'dolphin trainer's back.'

But after the zoo director delved into the keeper's work record, he found the only time he'd worked with aquatic animals, was a short stint with tropical fish.

When feeding the zoo inmates there was the ever-present gang of food groupies to contend with. Similar to the paparazzi that stalk celebrities. An assemblage of crows, seagulls, pigeons, sparrows, starlings and squirrels, shadowed me at feeding time. Determined to intercept food destined for the zoo inmates.

If I left food buckets unattended, even for a short time, these free loaders would dive into the smorgasbord in a feeding frenzy.

On my return, I would find obese wild birds, hurriedly waddling off, too heavy to become airborne. While bloated burping squirrels, like businessmen after a long lunch, staggered away supported by colleagues.

With the food rations now reduced by half, the hungry zoo inmates would protest in the only way they knew how, by attacking the waiter.

During my first winter at the zoo, fellow keepers wore so many clothes, their size, shape and sex, remained a mystery. In spring when the onion layers of attire were discarded, true identities were revealed, with some surprises.

The first job on dark winter mornings, was breaking ice covered water troughs in the enclosures to provide drinking water. And also breaking ice around the edges of ponds and lakes, to prevent foxes attacking wing clipped waterfowl on the ice.

This was a particularly difficult task for me to perform at Swan Lake, where one male black swan hated me with a vengeance. When I entered the lake enclosure, he emitted a piping call, reminiscent of a clarinet player, trying to find the right note. Then he'd make a bee-line for me, cutting through the water at speed.

Contrary to popular belief, swans can't break your legs with swipes from their wings. But if you're unprepared for an attack, they can easily knock you off balance. When you're being clouted by those powerful wings, it's hard to regain your footing. And deeply embarrassing, to be chased from an enclosure on your hands and knees, by what appears to be a large duck.

The black swan didn't have a mate. But he had a partner in crime. A large metallic green Muscovy duck, with blood shot eyes and a bright red face, reminiscent of a long-term whiskey drinker.

If the guy who designed the US president's bomb proof car, created a duck, it would be a Muscovy. Big and muscular, they are unlike any other duck. Forget Donald, think Arnie.

The male black swan's obsession with attacking me, was shared by the Muscovy. He had the unsavoury habit when the swan had rendered me horizontal of attempting to mate with my head. Every time I entered the enclosure, I was confronted with this pair of bully boys, intent on sex and violence.

To enable me to break the ice while avoiding Muscovy and swan attack, I placed generous amounts of corn in shallow water. This occupied them temporarily, as they had to submerge their heads to feed. But they would surface every few seconds, keeping me under surveillance.

One morning half asleep, having placed the corn in the water. I was enthusiastically jumping up and down on the ice when it broke. Descending, my Wellingtons rapidly filling with water, I was now wide awake, my teeth chattering like a football rattle. Dragging my half numb legs up the bank, occasionally slipping back into the water, the black swan seized his chance. Launching himself at me and whipping me relentlessly with his outstretched wings.

The Muscovy mounted my head, clasping his feet over my ears. I attempted to escape, but not very successfully. As I was walking on my knees in slippery conditions, wearing a duck on my head.

Periodically in the throes of passion, the Muscovy would grab tufts of hair, but the excitement was too much and eventually he fell off. Having worked up an appetite, sexually assaulting and beating me up, the duo resumed feeding on the submerged corn. Two ladies who witnessed the fracas, eyed me suspiciously.

"Why do you think the big black duck, was attacking the boy who has difficulty using his legs?' Her friend spoke loudly, for my benefit.

"Well it's obvious he must have taunted them at some time. You know what they say about ducks, they never forget."

Instructions on zoo feeding and cleaning routines were mind boggling. Made all the more complicated, by the fact that the head keeper and the second in charge senior keeper, had not spoken for six years. They communicated by leaving notes for each other, which after reading they angrily ripped up. I was used by both keepers as an intermediary and a conduit for their anger. Each one telling me to ignore the instructions the other one had just given me.

As an apprentice keeper, I always seemed to be carrying more items than a one-man band. Buckets, brushes, plus a whole range of unidentified cleaning implements, deemed essential but never used.

When the head keeper loaded you up with these items, he didn't stop till your legs started to bow. It was then and only then, you were handed the key ring.

This was so large, when I first saw it hung in the keeper's quarters I thought it was a hula-hoop.

"You'll get used to the keys son, after a week you won't notice them hanging on your belt."

I doubted it. Most of the older keepers resembled limping members of a prison chain gang. Who would easily qualify for hip transplants, due to years of having the equivalent of an anvil swinging from their belts.

I found the personal key collection a great hindrance. In winter they froze to my hand, or while swinging from my belt, got caught on the wire of a cage or enclosure. Jerking me backwards, jettisoning everything I was carrying skywards.

Some of the keys on the key ring were so old, they were for zoo buildings long since demolished. When I mentioned this, I was told obsolete keys were still on the key ring for sentimental reasons. One senior keeper took me aside to impart his words of wisdom. "You'll realise when you've been in this job a while, you can never have too many keys. Strength in numbers. Know what I mean?" (Not really, no)

On my first week at the zoo, during a lull in conversation at tea break. I naively suggested, why couldn't the locks be standardised? Then only one key would be required. This caused laughter, rolling around the floor and gripping ribs sort of laughter. When it subsided, the head keeper shaking his head, wiping tears from his eyes, placed a hand on my shoulder.

"Think about it son, you'd look a right idiot carrying a massive key ring around with just one key on it."

I only lost my key bunch once, but it was a memorable occasion.

SIEGE AT THE SEA LION POND

Like all young trainee keepers, I was moved around from one zoo section to another. When I had been terrorised and thoroughly bitten by one group of animals, I would be whisked off to receive the same treatment from another group of exotic thugs.

This week I was with the sea lions. Mac a serious talking Scot, who smelled strongly of fish, had a bushy grey and green moustache, which had evolved into separate facial hairy plantations covering both cheeks. The sides of his zoo uniform glistened with fluorescent fish scales, resulting from habitually thrusting his hands into his pockets. In the evening when he cycled home from the zoo, he didn't require lights. His iridescent uniform provided more than adequate illumination.

Mac wore Wellingtons winter and summer, with thick white fisherman's socks folded over the tops. The boots were at least one size too big. Consequently Mac's approach was always heralded by his rubbery footwear breaking wind. I once saw him on his day off in the local high street, dressed in shorts and trainers. I was convinced he had borrowed somebody else's legs for the day.

Mac proudly introduced me to his sea lions. The green water of the pond had a heavy swell, caused by the aquatic activity of these hyperactive marine mammals.

As we leaned over the wall, looking down into the enclosure, Mac spoke excitedly, punctuating his sentences by nudging me in the ribs.

"That's Barry. There's Max. Over there is Susie, isn't she a beauty? Yonder is young Freddie with the ball." Mac knew them individually like his own children. With animals you often establish

7

an immediate rapport. I instantly knew, they hated me. They gave me the look like bullies in the school playground, they were going to get me.

As Mac unlocked the sea lion enclosure, I couldn't have been any closer, if my feet had been inside his Wellingtons. "Listen laddie, rule number one, hang on to your keys. If you clip them on your belt these guys will have them away. They haven't got hands, but they don't need them. With their noses and teeth, they can open doors and turn keys in locks."

"I'll put them in my pocket," I suggested.

"These guys will empty your pockets quicker than a lassie on a Saturday night. You've got to grip your keys in your fist like this."

The keys disappeared into one of Mac's massive blotched hands.

"Always keep your bucket on your chest." He looked me up and down. "As you don't appear have a chest, stick it under your chin. That's to prevent the beasties diving in your bucket and having your fish away. The public don't like that, they come to see a professional performance."

The sea lions were now out of the water, weaving in and out of our legs like a pack of flippered wolves. I've never been a lover of marine animals. Or even animals associated with the sea, due to a traumatic experience I had as a child, on a seaside holiday in Blackpool.

I was on the beach, aboard a moth eaten donkey called Derek, who appeared to be hibernating standing up. When the donkey driver slapped Derek's backside he went from naught to snail pace. His front feet slowly moved forward, then his rear feet slowly moved backwards. He would then take a rest from the exertion. I would have made more progress aboard a statue.

Suddenly a transformation took place. As if prompted by an invisible sat nav, Derek faced the sea and inhaling the invigorating salty spray, clasped his front hooves together, launching himself headlong into the foamy waves.

I was frantically manoeuvring Derek's ears, trying to find reverse. But Derek, like a long eared Duncan Goodhew, was heading out to sea, on course for Dublin.

The sea lions were now jostling us like a crowd of shoppers at the summer sales. The algae covered rocks made it almost impossible to stand. I discovered later Mac's Wellingtons had metal studded soles, enabling him to remain confidently vertical. But I was like an out of control skater, gripping Mac's arm for support, my legs frantically moving in various directions.

"I can see you think this is easy." Mac said, as I shook my head vigorously, my feet exceeding the speed limit.

"Your goal is to reach the top of the pool, where at precisely 2.00pm you will perform the feeding of the sea lions.

But these guys are going to do all they can to stop you, by stealing your fish before you get there. So you have to be canny."

"How do I become canny Mac?"

"Don't speak! Sea lions never speak. That's not saying they don't understand every word we are saying. They are just as intelligent as you and I. In fact, I bet if they tried to speak they could." Mac was drifting into fan worship area.

Most senior keepers were prone to this, having formed a close bond with their animals over the years, they have an insight into that animal's behaviour and intelligence. But they are also often guilty of wildly overestimating the abilities of the animals in their care.

If Mac was allowed to drone on, he would soon be telling me, the sea lions climb out of the pool every evening to attend night school.

"Mac you were explaining how to feed the sea lions."

Mac was back.

"You have to distract them and buy time, throw them the odd fish to keep them at bay. To begin with, we throw a fish to Max, he's the dominant bull. Throw it to anybody else and you'll start a fight, as Max will assert his dominance. Watch! Here Max."

Mac threw a small fish on the grass at the far end of the enclosure. Max, the large bull sea lion, heavy and ungainly out of the water, made his way laboriously to retrieve it. Mac then threw more fish to other parts of the enclosure, calling each sea lion's name as he did so. The honking became deafening as each sea lion retrieved their fish. Mac made his way towards the pool's edge, apparently oblivious I was clinging to the tail of his jacket, legs apart being towed along.

"Watch Max, he'll bite your legs. But he's not as bad as Barry. Barry does-na let go when he bites. He's like a wee terrier with a rat."

Mac started to giggle, then slapped me in the middle of the back.

I circumnavigated him at speed, ending up tightly embracing his waist. I laughed, but fear prevented any sound emerging from me.

The sea lions were closing in again. Mac stood at the edge of the pool smiling, eyes closed, taking in a deep breath. "Fill your lungs with that sea air." (We were forty miles inland)

"You'll have to give me a moment laddie, I always get

emotional when I reach this spot. Twenty years ago my predecessor Crankie Crawford, was performing the throwing fish. He suffered a heart attack as he lobbed his last herring. Nose dived into the pool. It was the way he would have wanted to go. Crankie went down with his fish."

The sea lions were nudging and hassling us, while Mac wiped away his tears and composed himself for the performance. He took a large herring from the bucket and waved it above his head. The sea lions dived into the water, but not before one nipped my thigh.

"He bit me!" I shouted, rubbing my thigh vigorously.

Mac laughed.

"If that had been a real bite, you would have lost half your Wellington. Now pay attention! Let the performance begin. When you feed, make sure Susie gets her share, she's a wee bit shy see." Mac threw fish to each sea lion in turn.

The sea lions gulped down the herrings, honking eagerly, hoping for second helpings. Mac held the bucket upside down, before wiping his hands down the sides of his jacket.

"That's all gang."

As we walked back to the gate, I summoned all my skating skills and arrived there before Mac, running on the spot eager to be released.

I was so relieved at vacating sea lion territory, I started mouthing untruths.

"That was great Mac. I'd love to do it again, soon."

Mac slapped a massive herring smelling arm around my shoulder.

"Keen hey." I nodded as if my head was coming loose.

"Okay, you can feed them tomorrow on your own."

My grin faded, I swallowed audibly, the swallow of a frightened man.

"I may have to run through it a few more times Mac. It's a lot to take in. Would you consider a bribe?"

Mac couldn't hear, he was on autopilot.

"Remember always feed Max first, then Barry, Freddie and Bertha next and make sure Susie gets her share." Mac gave me a reassuring chiropractor style slap between the shoulder blades. "You've nothing to worry about laddie."

I forced a laugh, "I know, I'm probably being stupid. I mean what's the worse thing that can happen?"

I wish I hadn't asked, because Mac proceeded to tell me.

"That would be if two sea lions each grabbed one of your legs. Never let them do that, as they tend to chew." He lowered his gaze.

"At your nether regions. If you do collapse for any reason, keep smiling, try and make out its all part of the show. And never be fooled if any of the sea lions appear to be asleep. Sea lions can sleep with one eye open. They close one eye, resting one side of the brain. While keeping the other eye open and that side of the brain active. Then they alternate. It's called unihemispheric sleep."

"That's helpful," I muttered.

"By the way don't be tense or look scared, act confident. But don't be overconfident either, or they'll take you down a peg or two. Oh and watch out for seagulls."

"Do I have to feed them too?"

"No, but they'll swoop in from nowhere and steal your fish. Chill out Bill, just relax and enjoy the experience. Now I better show you where the nearest first aid box is."

The blood had left my face. Tomorrow, I was convinced it would vacate the rest of my body.

I awoke the next day, having spent the night tormented by an awful dream. Max and Barry were towing me around the sea lion pool. Each of them had one of my legs in their mouths. All the people I admired and girls I wanted to impress were in the front row. To add to my embarrassment, all I was wearing was Wellingtons and my zoo keeper's hat.

At breakfast I prayed for rain. The crowds would stay away. I could then throw the fish over the wall of the sea lion enclosure and nobody would know. If the creator could arrange for a thunderstorm around 3.00pm sea lion feeding time, I would be eternally grateful.

I prayed, oh did I pray. I promised to always watch "Songs of Praise" and buy Cliff Richards CD's. But big G had left the receiver off the hook. The day turned out to be a real scorcher. The weather attracted the crowds like a free pop concert. With a heavy heart, I collected the bucket of herrings from the zoo food store.

The fish looked exactly as I felt. Mac had loaned me a pair of his Wellingtons. Although they were two sizes too big, they had metal studded soles. I might be savaged to death, but I would remain vertical throughout the ordeal.

By the time I reached the venue I had a posse of sea lion groupies around me and a massive crowd ringed the enclosure. As I squeezed my way through a chant rang out.

"He's going to feed them. He's going to feed them."

One wise person interjected. "You wouldn't get me in there."

I hurriedly unlocked the gate, while the sea lions were still in the water.

Before I knew it, a pimple faced sea lion groupie, wearing an anorak held together with animal welfare badges, was trying to enter the enclosure alongside me.

I squeezed in, while prizing her out.

"Can you confirm that your fish are humanely killed?"

"I can, we only use fish that have collapsed."

I managed to close the gate with Miss Anorak on the outside.

She leaned over the fence. "What do you say, when I tell you all meat is murder? "

"I would say find a new butcher."

Gripping my keys tightly, with my bucket under my chin, I was shuffling along in heavy Wellingtons, which I realised were on the wrong feet.

I made my way across the enclosure, ready for anything, apart from what was about to befall me.

One minute the sea lions were in the water, gazing at me like a group of big-eyed scuba divers. Next thing they were conducting a body search with cold wet noses.

I banged the bucket against my head, just on the off chance I was in another dream. A lump arose on my forehead. No such luck, I started to slowly make my way towards the pool. That's when I felt nips on the backs of my legs. The nips became more frequent. I tried to vary my steps to avoid bites. I body swerved, sold the odd dummy, even skipped a lengthy excerpt from 'Riverdance.'

The crowd applauded, in appreciation of this bizarre bucket-wielding tap dancer. I suddenly remembered I should be throwing fish. I'd been having such a good time I'd forgotten the sea lion's names. I threw a fish to Barry

"There you go Boris." Barry completely ignored the fish and looked around for the new sea lion. A fish disappeared down my Wellington. Holding the bucket high, I tried to dislodge it holding my leg aloft, shaking it hokey cokey style. The fish dropped out when my Wellington came off. The sea lions watched it tumble down the rocks into the pool.

I lowered the bucket for an instant, to pull one soggy sock up and two sleek black heads dived into the bucket of fish, pulling me over in the process. Then my remaining Wellington came off and joined its colleague in the pool.

I retained possession of the bucket. Curling around it foetal style, clutching my keys. The sea lions encircled me, occasionally nudging me with a wet nose, or wiping my face with a flipper. One was concerned enough to lay alongside, attempting to revive me by breathing fish fumes in my face. A shout from the front row brought me back to reality. "Are you going to feed them or not?"

My audience was waiting. I brushed flippers aside and rose to my feet. Hoisting the bucket high, I started to goose step through the sea lion congregation. They followed, once more biting my legs, or pulling at the two foot lengths of sock hanging from each foot.

Fatigue was setting in, as it does when you're losing blood, but the mission had to be accomplished. I muttered Mac's instructions. "Act confident." The sea lions continued to nip my legs. "But not too confident." They still nipped my legs.

In a daze I threw fish over my shoulder at a rapidly increasing rate. The sea lions gulped down the fish, then resumed devouring my lower limbs.

Legs quaking, with the bucket lodged under my chin, I finally reached the edge of the pool. I swayed on the precipice. The sea lions were in the water, bobbing up and down, performing synchronised food queuing.

The people began to cheer. I was moved. They were applauding my success at running the gauntlet. I had been wrestled to the ground, repeatedly bitten, lost my footwear, all in the line of duty. But my bucket of fish and keys, were still in my possession. What a pro. All I had to do now was perform the throwing of the fish and the ordeal would be over. Gripping my keys firmly in one hand, my other hand searched frantically around in the bucket for fish.

Peering down. Two small sprats, three eyes between them peered back. The most pathetic performance of a lifetime was about to commence. Hoping to disguise that the sea lions were on extremely low rations. I threw the fish quickly in the air shouting a string of names.

"Tom, Dick, Harry, feeding time. Enjoy!"

It's one of those moments I often relive. A sea of faces and five open mouthed sea lions, watched two small fish grabbed in mid air by a swooping one-legged seagull. While a bunch of keys hurtled through the air and disappeared into the water.

There have been better days.

ATTACKED BY A FURRY JUMPER

One aspect all zoo keepers hate about their job, is being gawped at by members of the public, while working in a zoo enclosure. You might say that a window dresser has a similar problem, but window dressers are never attacked by store mannequins.

I was always warned by the more experienced keepers, if ever I was set upon by an angry, or what was more likely a sex crazed animal, not to expect sympathy from zoo visitors. It's that affinity zoos have with menageries, harking back to the gory days, when wild beasts fought gladiators in the Roman arena. The public will be unable to perceive you are being attacked. You're part of the entertainment!

As a young apprentice keeper, I prayed if it was my fate to ever fall prey to a zoo inmate, to please let it happen before opening time. To go through my death throes, in full view of an audience of ice cream licking visitors, didn't bear thinking about.

People often classify animals into friendly and non-friendly. We have those fearsome beasts that disgrace themselves on wildlife documentaries, killing and mating without restraint. Generally behaving like animals and the others, who appear to have been designed by mutual agreement between Walt Disney and Mothercare. Surprisingly, some of the most innocent looking and cuddly animals, turn out to be the most belligerent.

Koalas eat a diet so low in nutrients, they sleep up to twenty hours a day.

Their name is aboriginal for 'no drink.' They do drink, but are so lethargic, by the time they climb down to a waterhole, it's usually dried up, or a shopping mall has been built on it.

Because koalas possess cute faces and have noses that appear to have been sewn on, they are assumed to be furry toys that live in trees, adorable and pick-up-able. Pick one up and they smell like they have been dead for a fortnight, leak strong smelling urine and when you attempt to put them down, they grip you with claws like Freddie Kruger.

If a koala happens to die in your arms, which they have been known to do out of spite. Be prepared to be lumbered with it for a long time, as koalas don't relax their grip when they die. Before they were protected and hunted for fur, inexperienced hunters found bagging a koala often meant going home empty handed. After shooting one that was seated comfortably in a tree, it usually stayed seated comfortably in the tree.

The largest four legged Australian, the Red Kangaroo, is generally regarded as friendly and helpful, thanks to over acting by sixties marsupial TV star Skippy. Unable to walk or run, kangaroos have developed hopping to an Olympian standard. Once on the move they can reach speeds of 35 mph, jumping distances of up to thirty feet and changing direction with ease.

Kangaroos continue to grow throughout their life, becoming stronger and more cantankerous with age and they just love to fight.

Two males engaged in a contest, will lean backwards balancing on their tails and strike at each other with their hind feet. While also using their strong forelimbs to pull their opponent towards them. This natural tendency to spar with the forelimbs, is how the term 'boxing kangaroo' originated. Kangaroos are also not averse to using weapons. Bushmen carrying a stick for protection, against a large male, 'old man' kangaroo have sometimes found the tables turned when the kangaroo has grabbed the stick and used it to attack them.

In my youthful naivety, all I knew when I became a zoo keeper was kangaroos jump and they have a waistcoat pocket that doubles as a nursery. I was totally unaware they were skilled in the art of unarmed combat.

As we entered a kangaroo enclosure at Taronga Zoo, Sydney's famous zoo that overlooks Sydney harbour. Dave my little Welsh colleague, mysteriously known as Ducky, warned me, "Watch out for the old man."

"What old man?" I enquired, seeing only a group of sandy red coloured kangaroos sleeping soundly. The only indication of life being their twitching ears keeping flies at bay.

Dave nodded his head jerkily in their direction.

"The old man roo, the large one in the corner, if he gets up, we get out."

The large animal in question was sleeping deeply, his stomach slowly rising and falling. Dave nervously began to sweep the enclosure, never taking his eyes off the kangaroo. I was just relaxed, enjoying the morning sunshine.

As is often the case, when you are sweeping animal manure, a wave of happiness will waft over you. As it wafted over me, I started to whistle. Dave ran over and grabbed my sleeve.

"Don't!"

"Don't what?"

"Don't whistle, the old man doesn't like whistling."

Dave was tense as a snake charmer with a broken flute. But I was unaware of any danger. Suddenly the sleeping kangaroo awoke. "Oh now you've done it boyo. Now you've done it."

I thought Dave had disappeared, then I realised he had jumped behind me, his quivering finger sticking out under my ear. It was pointing at the large kangaroo, who was now vertical, his barrel chest thrust forward threateningly.

He snorted and a flock of sparrows feeding on grain in the kangaroo's food trough, simultaneously took flight scattering the husks.

I could see the kangaroo's forelimbs were equipped with long black claws, which he was using to scratch his chest, or perhaps he was sharpening them?

"What do we do now?" I whispered out of the side of my mouth.

"Don't know, he's never stood up before. I've always been told never whistle and if he stands up, try and be somewhere else."

When you are in the enclosure of an aggressive animal that wants to assert dominance, forget the teachings of Dr Dolittle, just use the exit. The primal instinct to protect one's home ground is ingrained in all living things. It's the root cause of conflicts, such as neighbours squabbling over parking places and the occasional world war. Try pacifying an animal on his territory and you'll soon be horizontal on a hospital trolley.

Dave was now clutching the back of my shirt and twisting it in a knot. As if by unspoken agreement we started to move backwards.

"You must have some idea what to do," I said, as we shuffled along gaining speed like children playing at trains.

"After all, you're an experienced kangaroo keeper."

"I'm more of a duck man really, that's why they call me Ducky Thomas. I've never been a natural with kangaroos. There's not a lot of call for it in Wales."

With an effortless bound, the kangaroo jumped towards us grinding his teeth. Dave was clinging to my back like a stranded mountaineer on a rock face. As the kangaroo got nearer Dave wailed. "He's coming! He's closing in for the kill."

We accelerated chugging backwards.

The kangaroo jumped forwards again. Dave squealed. "They've killed people in Queensland."

"Calm down, we're in New South Wales."

"Do you think he's influenced by geography?"

As soon as we got a reasonable distance from this belligerent Aussie, he performed a couple of hops and he was upfront and personal again.

I had a plan, according to Sir David Attenborough all species bluff more than attack, call their bluff and they usually retreat. I took two steps forward, with Dave in tow. Then I took another two steps forward. The kangaroo hopped to meet us. We were only a yard apart. He obviously hadn't heard about bluff theory, or chose to ignore it.

I could smell his breath. It was a safe bet he didn't floss. If he jumped now he'd flatten us and I didn't have Sir David's number.

Suddenly Dave the little Welsh fireball erupted.

"That's quite enough. I refuse to be terrorised by an animal with a pouch."

Dave leapt from behind me, holding up his clenched fists, skipping back and forth with reasonable impressive footwork, only occasionally tripping himself up.

"You overgrown Australian hamster. If it's a fight you want, I'll give you a fight. Put em up." The kangaroo held his head back, growling, thrusting his chest out.

Dave picked up a broom and thrust it at the kangaroo. He clearly disliked this and turned his head away snorting. Dave held the broom at the furry Aussie's chest and lunged forward with all his might, shunting the kangaroo backwards. Dave repeated this and the kangaroo was pushed back even further. You're winning Dave I thought. "You're a fake aren't you boyo?" Dave was pumped up.

"Typical Australians .You love chucking your weight around. But you don't like it when the tables are turned." Dave lunged again with the broom. It seemed Dave had called his bluff. The kangaroo was steadily retreating.

Dave turned to me his broom poised for another assault.

"He's nothing but an overgrown gerbil really. All these years they have been winding me up about him. They even nicknamed him Mangler."

What happened next, happened so fast, it took my breath away. It had exactly the same effect on Dave. The kangaroo performed a series of movements with such dexterity, that they looked like rehearsed martial art moves. Pure poetry in violence. First the broom was wrenched from Dave's hands, then he was clouted over the head with it. While clutching his head, he was kicked in the chest with what I must admit was an excellent drop kick. Laughter erupted from a group of visitors who had gathered to watch this gladiatorial bout. Dave winded and dazed, scurried away on his hands and knees muttering.

"I'll see you later."

The kangaroo turned and faced me, obviously thinking, one down, one to go. I quickly ran over to the wheelbarrow and crouched down behind it. How keen was a kangaroo's eyesight? At first he didn't appear to realise I was behind the barrow. Then with a couple of bounds and a swift movement of one forelimb, he effortlessly swept the barrow aside exposing a shaking zoo keeper. I smiled and grabbed the broom. But quickly discarded it, after remembering what had happened to Dave when he was armed with it.

I've always held the opinion that a vegetarian lifestyle engenders feelings of altruism. But this vegan looked mean and menacing. Perhaps it's their lonely childhood that makes kangaroos so aggressive. A month after conception, blind and hairless, they are evicted from the womb.

As if that isn't enough of a trauma. Blind and hairless they have to climb unaided through a hairy belly, that must seem like a mountainous rain forest. Eventually they reach the skyscraper playroom known as the pouch and with no say in the matter are christened Joey.

Dave was pulling himself up into a standing position, clinging to the gate of the enclosure. He then posed, with one hand on his hip and a shaky smile on his dust covered face.

Characteristically he was trying to impress the public that wrestling with a kangaroo was a daily occurrence. I thought he may return to assist me, as camaraderie among zoo keepers is a strong bond. Unfortunately the survival instinct is stronger and Dave quickly scrambled over the gate to safety. Hopefully he would soon return with help.

The crowd around the enclosure appeared satisfied with the morning's entertainment. I suppose they assumed we were the warm up act prior to the lions being fed. Any minute now I'm going to be launched into orbit by those ten inch long feet. Each possessing an elongated fourth toe and equally long toenail, with which kangaroos can inflict serious damage. What could I do? I decided to use my in depth knowledge of animal behaviour. I would try and scare the kangaroo by shouting loudly. I had sound scientific basis that this would work. I had seen it in a Tarzan film. I filled my lungs to capacity and raised my head.

"Here goes. Ar-gh-gh-gh, Argh-gh-gh-gh." My face went red then blue, my body shook and my toes started to curl. "Argh-gh-gh-gh-gh!"

Birds evacuated trees. It was a sound to rival any banshee's wail. I continued yelling till my lungs were depleted of air. I was drained and I had almost deafened myself.

The kangaroo never blinked an eyelid. I wonder whatever happened to Tarzan? I believe he was massacred by kangaroos.

All eyes of the crowd were now on me, the game was almost over. The outcome was to be decided by penalty kicks and I was the ball. The kangaroo growled and scraped his chest with his claws, followed by a kind of Ali shuffle. He then looked me up and down, clenching his claws and sticking his bum out Johnny Wilkinson style.

He took a long sniff at the breeze, obviously calculating given the wind direction, how far he could kick me. My only hope was Dave would soon return with help.

But that hope was dashed, when I spotted him in the crowd

stood in between two Japanese tourists, having his photo taken.

The kangaroo now had the look that wrestlers have during their pre-match interview, when their medication has worn off. Suddenly the wheelbarrow fell over with a loud clunk. The roo's ears twitched

He pivoted on his long tail and snorted at the wheelbarrow.

Hoisting it up, he threw his head back and attempted to use the mangled object as a pair of chest expanders. Kangaroos can jump thirty feet when they are on the move. I appeared to do that from a standing position, landing near the gate of the enclosure. Dave interrupting filming, rushed to let me out. As if things weren't bad enough, He decided to play to the gallery.

"How many times have I told you to keep your eyes on the animals when you're working in an enclosure?" He then turned to the crowd shaking his head, "These trainees have a lot to learn."

This wasn't very convincing, coming from a man whose shirt was missing a sleeve and had two large kangaroo footprints stamped on the front. Since that assault with a deadly marsupial, I have only one thing to say when people talk about kangaroos. Skippy was a white wash.

DRINKING WITH THE HAIRY BOYS

As a trainee zoo keeper, I had just completed two weeks of bliss on the bird section. Birds are among my favourites and rarely attack. Okay, if you sunbathe naked in the vulture enclosure you might be pushing it a bit, especially with my anaemic complexion. But compared with many other species, they are amiable and largely inoffensive. After bidding farewell to feathered and featherless friends at the Bird House. I next joined the team on the primate section. I made the mistake of calling it "The Ape House." Which made all the staff there go ape-well unhappy.

In this establishment lived chimps, gorillas and orang-utans. The latter being large long haired orange apes from Indonesia, who resemble spruced up new age travellers.

The first aggressive hairy primate I met up with was Gerald, the head keeper whose beard looked as if it had been knitted not grown. Gerald detested bird keepers, referring to me as the budgie minder. He was also a bully. My first day he filled my lunch box with gorilla dung and told me it was homework.

One of my tasks at the Ape House, was to give the chimps their afternoon drink of blackcurrent juice. This was passed to them through the 'chimp pipe.' A six inch diameter pipe in the wall, linking the food preparation room with the chimp's outdoor enclosure. It was important to keep a firm grip on the cup. Allowing each chimp to take a drink, without them being able to grab the cup. The chimps would usually take it in turns to take a sip. But occasionally, one would use his sink plunger shaped lips to siphon all the juice in one go. I would then have to pull with some effort, to extricate chimp lips from cup. In between the rounds of drinks, the chimps eyed me suspiciously through the pipe. Baring their teeth, or making whoopee cushion noises. Behaving pretty much like any other group of afternoon drinkers.

Chimps share 98% of our DNA and are our closest living relatives. So it's no surprise they are the bovver boys of the primate world. Most people are familiar with young chimps, with their big rubbery ears, large sad eyes and hair parted smartly in the middle. When playing they will nibble your nose, while pulling on your ears, to see what kind of response they get. But they are mischievous without being malevolent.

An adult chimp by contrast, is big mean and menacing, much stronger than a man. Chimps have hospitalised humans numerous times. And worse. If you had a nightclub in the jungle, you might consider having a gorilla on the door. But he's a softie. An adult chimp would afford better security. The only trouble is, he wouldn't let anybody in, or out.

One afternoon as usual, I was on juice detail. But unusually there was no sign of the chimps. I repeatedly called out "c'mon guys." While pushing the cup further out of the pipe, thinking they were probably at the other end of the enclosure. I knew differently, when my wrist was gripped firmly. I could hear chimp chatter, on the other side of the wall, loosely translated, it sounded like:

"We've caught the budgie minder."

What was I going to do? If I shouted for help they might get agitated. I felt my arm being tugged, not hard, just enough to let me know, it would either come away from the socket easily. Or that I could be effortlessly pulled through the pipe to join them. I tried to relax, breathe deeply, stay calm, while rapidly reciting a prayer. I pondered on my predicament.

Would I end up being the only zoo keeper with one arm five feet long?

If that happened, I'd have to let them stretch the other arm or I would look ridiculous. What was I talking about? With both arms five feet long I would still look ridiculous. I came out of this meditative trance, when a warm wet tongue started licking my hand. The licking became more intense, I could feel teeth nibbling and there was a whole mouth full of them. I pleaded, "Please don't eat the hand." This was a hostage situation, yet I didn't even know what their demands were. A plane to Africa, a banana plantation of their choice?

The hand licking stopped, followed by more screeching. Another chimp took over, introducing himself with a firm handshake, the handshakes increased. I felt like Prince Phillip on a busy day. Now more than one chimp was gripping my hand. I was under no illusions of the danger. Chimps don't just sit around eating bananas, discussing tea blends, or dreaming of running away to join the circus. Wild chimps will hunt down and kill monkeys and other animals. Inter group rivalry can also result in chimp killing chimp. Yet for a long time their carnivorous tendencies were unknown or disbelieved.

On their island enclosure in the zoo, chimps would occasionally catch water hens and ducks, who had ventured too close. This would shock visitors, who expect to see chimps sucking oranges or chewing bananas, not sitting cross-legged leisurely plucking a duck. But like us, they are hunters at heart. Although we have largely redirected our hunting instincts, into wandering aimlessly around shopping malls.

My captors were now getting loud and agitated. Perhaps arguing over ownership of the captured limb? It went quiet; perhaps they had come to a decision, decided to share portions and were forming an orderly queue. Teeth were now nibbling my fingernails. At least I had the perfect alibi for having my arm lodged in the pipe. I was having a chimp manicure. At that moment, the door opened. Oh why did it have to be po-faced Gerald? He eyed me scornfully, which was how he usually viewed me.

"I've got a hand problem Gerald."

"What sort of hand problem?"

"The hand I used to have, the chimps have got it."

"How the hell did they get your hand?"

"It was holding the cup."

"What have you been taught?" Any second he was going to ask me about the golden rule. He never failed to ask about the golden rule when you put a foot wrong. He stabbed his finger in my direction.

"What is the golden rule all zoo keepers should abide by? "

I mumbled head bowed in shame.

"Never ever deviate from the routine. Stick to the routine and you will be safe." (God bless the golden rule and all who sail in her.)

Gerald strutted around the room, shaking his head. Now he was going to tell me his employment history.

"I've been working with chimps for six years. I spend valuable time passing on my experience to the likes of you and what do you do? "

"I ignore it." I muttered.

"Yes you ignore it!" Gerald slumped down in a chair and opened his newspaper.

"Gerald, is there any chance of persuading the chimps to release what is left of my arm? " Gerald flicked through newspaper.

"You trainees are a waste of oxygen."

The chimps were sucking my fingers again, my arm was numb, or perhaps all that was left was fingers! In the same way that amputees experience the ghost of the limb. Did I have fingers on the end of a virtual arm?

Without looking up Gerald yelled, "Jimbo, Johnny, leave it!"

My arm was suddenly released. I quickly pulled it from the pipe and checked to see if it was longer than the one that had evaded capture. I was relieved it was the correct length, but rigidly horizontal, I felt like a traffic policeman after a long shift.

He sniffed "You're on the lions next week. Carry on ignoring procedure and we'll be seeing a lot less of you in future."

He sniggered and as usual his nostrils flared like a warthog encountering a bad smell. Begrudgingly I smiled and thanked my rescuer.

"Thanks Gerald."

The only way I could do this, was by imagining good old Gerald, reading his paper, mumbling into his knitted beard, while being pulled feet first through the chimp pipe.

Despite sharing a common ancestor with chimps and having a similar hairstyle, I have never kept in touch with those African relatives, nor had drinks with them since that day.

PIGS MIGHT FLY

I was around twenty, sharing a house with several other young trainee zoo keepers, trying to make ends meet on the meagre wages that zoos used to pay. As all young people do when they house share, we would sit up till the early hours of the morning righting the world's wrongs. The naive idealism of youth, coupled with endless energy and optimism, meant we had solutions to every global problem by the time the last bottle of cider was finished.

A favourite subject for the after hours discussion group, was the virtues of the vegetarian lifestyle. We were all vegetarians albeit through necessity, living as we did on such culinary combinations as porridge and beans and what fruit we could wrestle off the zoo animals. The contents of the fridge had long since been consumed. Real food was something we aspired to acquire in the more affluent future.

One particular night as cheap cider flowed, the moral arguments supporting vegetarianism were greeted with much smug nodding approval. Until, someone mentioned the pig! We all hung our heads in shame.

Here we were pontificating about a meat free life style and yet we were aiding and abetting the demise of an innocent pig, due to celebrate Christmas by being eaten at the festive barbeque.

"How could we be so hypocritical?"

"We must save the pig."

"When?"

"What about tonight?"

"Its the security guard's night off."

"Then what are we waiting for?"

"Let's do it."

Nobody dared disagree. Although there was no security present in the zoo grounds, the risks were still very great. If we were caught, we would lose our jobs and our careers would be ruined.

Convinced we were on the threshold of becoming the next Gerald Durrell or David Attenborough, there was a lot at stake.

Ropes and torches for the mercy mission were hastily collected. We also required some nutritional enticement. One member of the pig catching team mentioned pigs love truffles. Considering we couldn't even afford mushroom soup, this was of little help. We planned to tempt the pink beast with apples. We had a sack of windfalls collected from the garden. There was also a large wedge of wedding cake, which for the past six months had been posing as a doorstop.

After loading the pig catching kit into our un-roadworthy vehicle, we made our way along the deserted roads to the zoo. The plan, if you can call it that, was to hoist the pig over the wall using a rope. First we had to get pig to the wall from his quarters in the children's zoo. We managed this by enticing him with apples. Holding them a few inches from his nose like the proverbial carrot and a stick. He walked and gulped them down, one after another. It was like loading a blender. But if the apple supply was interrupted he refused to move a trotter.

Arriving at the perimeter wall, a rope was tied around him like a body harness. The other end, was thrown over the wall to a rope man waiting in the zoo car park, who then commenced to hoist the pig. Everything was going according to plan. But as soon as pig's feet left terra firma, he started to squeal. In the quiet hours of the morning he was as loud as a car alarm. Other zoo inmates joined in. Pig only stopped squealing when lowered back to the ground.

When lifted off the ground he would again voice his disapproval. An increasing number of zoo voices would then join in the shambolic chorus of "Old Macdonald's farm."

"We can't hoist him over the wall while he's making that noise."

"If he could feel something under his feet, maybe, just maybe, he would think he was still on the ground and remain silent." We found some small planks of wood and tied his feet to these. When we hoisted him up, he remained silent and apparently contented, just like your average pig on a skiing holiday.

But securing planks to trotters is difficult. When he began to shake and wriggle in mid air, they fell off. Devoid of these, he squealed till he was lowered to the ground.

"What if he was wearing shoes?"

"Or boots. There are Wellingtons in the car."

The Wellingtons were hastily fitted on pig. I had to confess I had never bought Wellingtons for a pig, but these looked far too big. Fortunately we had some thick socks and after fitting these on the trotters the boots fitted a treat.

The rope man went into action and pig in boots ascended the wall, grunting softly, with single grunts, coinciding with each jerk of the rope. When pig reached the top of the wall, the rope man climbed over the wall ready to lower pig into the zoo car park. Pig was silent, so far so good.

Suddenly there were headlights approaching. We shouted to the rope man to stop lowering. Pig was now suspended three quarters of the way up the wall, fortunately hidden in darkness. Everybody in the car park scurried into nearby bushes. The car came to a halt. The driver got out and stood looking in our direction.

Being caught red-handed pig stealing, was an offence punishable by having your roof set on fire and your goats and wife confiscated. That's in New Guinea, but it illustrates the seriousness of the offence

The man fumbled in the inside pocket of his jacket, producing a long cigar. He lit it and we held our breath as he walked determinedly towards us. He stumbled and changed direction, now walking towards the wall. From his unsteady gait, it was obvious he was more than a little worse for wear. Fumbling with his trousers he arrived at the wall. Leaning on one outstretched hand, steam rising, he christened the brickwork. He hadn't seen us. He wasn't the only one who was relieved. Hopefully when he had finished, he would make his way back to his car and depart, leaving us to continue with our rescue mission.

The last thing you would expect, when you are involved in a private function, in a deserted car park, in the early hours of the morning- happened!

The rope slipped through the fingers of tired rope man. The pig descended at speed and pinned our shocked urinator to the ground.

I could just see the news headlines. "Zoo keepers on the run, after man is mysteriously killed by falling pig. Police convinced it has all the signs of a contract killing."

As Pig sat comfortably astride the man's back, the victim suddenly moved. Wriggling out from under his pink assailant he sat upright, breathing heavily.

The cigar still between his lips now resembled a brown rosette. He got to his feet, as did the pig, who wagged his tail the Wellingtons pivoting on all four feet.

The man spat out the cigar. "You're wearing Wellingtons." The pig looked proudly at his footwear. The man shaking his head staggered back to his vehicle.

Sitting in the car he closed his eyes, before vigorously slapping his face. "There are no pigs, there are no pigs." The pig was now being frantically hoisted up the wall, while the drunken man still arguing with himself, was making his way back from the car. When he reached the scene of the assault, pig was suspended directly above him in darkness. We held our breath, if pig started to grunt we were history. Our friend dropped to his knees and parted the grass.

"That's more like it, not one pig wearing Wellingtons in sight."

He made his way back to the car. Starting the engine, the headlights illuminated the car park, as the vehicle turned and roared off leaving us once again in the darkness.

The pig was lowered back down the wall. Bundling him hurriedly into the back seat of the car, we drove away, mission accomplished.

Heading back to the house we were hyper with excitement, relief and accomplishment. We congratulated ourselves on a job well done. Until somebody enquired:

"What are we going to do with the pig?"

Pig stared at us expectantly.

"We could release him."

"Where?"

"On a farm somewhere."

"You mean a pig farm? He would be eaten."

Back at the house we sat around in a circle on the floor. The pig was asleep on the couch, snoring as you would expect, like a pig.

It was five in the morning. We had made one a big mistake when we abducted the pig. We shouldn't have done it. The bright spark who first suggested rescuing the pig, had a new suggestion.

"Why not take him back to the zoo? After all we have made our point."

Everybody agreed. The murmur went round the room.

"That's true."

"He's right."

What point we had made, apart from demonstrating that we could hoist a pig over a wall and drop him on a urinating drunk, was not clear. The pig somehow realising that he was not staying, awoke, jumped from the couch and circled the room grunting.

All those squeals that had been suppressed during the kidnap started to surface. He squealed as if he was trying to contact pigs on other continents. We tried to silence him with apples, but considering he had eaten the equivalent of a small orchard, he declined the offer. The squealing continued. He raised his head trying to find higher notes. Lights went on in neighboring houses. Pig had beaten every alarm clock in the neighborhood. We wrestled him on to the settee, trying to stifle his cries with cushions, when there was a loud knock at door.

"Good God, I hope they haven't called the police."

We opened the door, relieved to see one of our friendly neighbours, in his dressing gown on the doorstep.

We greeted him over the pig's squeals.

"Morning Mr. Garstang, So how's things?"

Mr Garstang minus his glasses, failed to recognize a pig seated on the settee, sandwiched in the middle of a group of smiling youths.

(Easily identifiable, as he was only one without long hair and a beard.)

"I don't want to interfere, but could you try and give your baby a bottle or something? He's ever so loud."

"No problem Mr Garstang. He's just visiting and we will be taking him back to the zoo. I mean his home very soon, which is most definitely not the zoo."

We had to get pig back to the zoo before his absence was discovered. But we couldn't risk hoisting him back over the wall.

It was now light and we would be seen. There was only one solution; we would leave him tied up at the entrance of the zoo, to be found by the first member of staff who turned up for work. And that's how in 1972, one December morning, a pig without Wellingtons, was found at the main entrance of Taronga Park Zoo, Sydney.

The social club Christmas party went off a treat. As usual at Christmas when free food was on offer, we were transformed from vegetarians into enthusiastic carnivores and enjoyed a very pleasant barbecue. The pig came too.

CATCHING THE HIGH SPEED RAIL

Apart from the ostrich and the other long legged avian athletes, there are other birds that are as fast on two legs as they are on the wing.

With a lightweight skeleton and wings to assist body swerving, a grounded bird is no fish out of water. Even chickens can out pace their owner, especially when the word drumsticks is mentioned. The ground cuckoo known as a Roadrunner made famous by the cartoon character, competes with cars on US desert highways. Pulling up alongside them at traffic lights. Taunting drivers, by staring them out and making revving noises.

Lesser-known speed merchants are waterhens and rails. Waterhens are hindered somewhat by their long toes and in a hurry, resemble someone trying to jog in skis. Some island species of rails have evolved into flightless birds and these are the fleetest of foot. Among them is New Zealand's Weka Rail. As a rookie keeper at one English zoo there was a notoriously speedy Weka Rail, who was deservedly nick-named Blur. His mate had died and we were desperately trying to find him another one.

Blur occupied an aviary in a large tropical house. At the rear of his aviary was a passageway that ran the length of the building, with a exit door leading outside. Walking down the passageway was treacherous. The chimps inside quarters was directly above and due to shoddy building work, gaps had been left which enabled hairy arms and rubber lipped faces to appear. Having your collar felt and hair pulled was a regular event.

To avoid chimp manhandling, keepers negotiated the passageway like a team of Quasimodo impersonators. The passageway lights were always turned off before entering the aviaries, to prevent birds escaping into the passageway. But sometimes keepers forgot. And this is how Blur ended up doing laps of the passage, cheered on, by rows of upside down faces of man's closet relatives. The rail sprinted back and forth along the corridor, so fast there appeared to be more than one bird. Two keepers with nets, positioned themselves at either end of the passageway. Like tennis players minus the ball, using dexterous overhead and backhand strokes, accompanied by grunts that would embarrass Sharapova, they attempted to net the elusive bird. Even when netted, Blur shot out of the net as quick as he shot in, leaving the puzzled keeper checking the net for holes.

The rail never slowed down, demonstrating his agility by running along the walls, just as speedily as he legged it along the ground. He then stopped in front of one of the keepers as if taunting him. The keeper raised his net slowly above his head.

Cometh the hour cometh the man.

Right hour, wrong man.

The exhausted keeper toppled backwards, while the rail embarked on a lap of honour.

Breathlessly one of the keepers suggested.

"You know what we need"

"Oxygen and a gun!"

"Extra help, open the door just a small gap and see if there is anybody there."

The keeper complied, but the small gap from which sunlight beamed was sufficient for the Weka Rail to make a swift exit. The indoor jaunt had now turned into a cross-country event.

But the rail had not disappeared as we first thought; he was circumnavigating the perimeter wall of 'Chimp Island,' the circular moated island housing the African hairy boys.

Clutching our nets we pursued the winged athlete as the chimps performed a Mexican wave. But completely exhausted we were running on empty. At one point the rail came running towards us. Confused, we turned and ran off with Blur in pursuit. It was ten minutes to zoo opening time; we would soon be participating in an embarrassing spectator sport.

We were so fatigued, we could hardly stand and slumped down against the chimp wall, while every few minutes Blur sprinted past.

"You'll never catch him like that boys." Between bouts of coughing and waving away clouds of pipe smoke, Barney a grizzled old zoo keeper appeared on the scene and as always was generous with his advice.

"You just need to assist him to find his way home."

"What do you mean, draw him a map, call him a cab, what kind of advice is that Barney?"

"Your first mistake was closing the door to his aviary. Open that, then open the door to the passageway leaving the light on. We herd him towards the passageway entrance, as soon as he enters the passageway switch the passage light off. He'll then enter the only illuminated area, his aviary."

"How can you be so sure he'll do that Barney?"

"That's how we've always got him back. But when you closed his aviary door, what should have been a walk in the park became a marathon."

Following Barney's instructions, Blur was soon back in his aviary. Just as the head keeper phoned.

"I hear the Weka Rail got out."

"Out! well I suppose technically he was out. Birds always head for the light as we all know, so we turned off the lights in the passageway. After hopping out of his aviary he simply hopped back in.

"Well done. Don't forget to retrieve your nets."

"Nets!"

"The ones you dropped when the Weka Rail was chasing you around Chimp Island.

GREAT ESCAPES AND
RHEA RACING

Catching birds and animals involves many tried and tested techniques. All animals are individuals and what might work with one animal doesn't work with another. Many a green horn zoo keeper has tried to restrain an animal and ended up with the animal restraining them.

It's therefore imperative to have knowledge of the animal's capabilities, before attempting to capture it.

As an apprentice keeper working in the zoo aquarium, I was instructed to transfer a group of piranhas to a larger tank, as overcrowded fish have a tendency to fight and often kill their colleagues.

I chose a light net that I could deftly manoeuvre in the water and demonstrate my fishing skills to the audience of aquarium keepers.

Piranha are well known for their ferocity and ability to quickly reduce animals that end up in the water into skeletons. These exploits have been exaggerated and although they do have unusually sharp teeth, they are mainly scavengers feeding on dead animals. Injuries to humans mainly occur, when swimmers or bathers unwittingly get too close to a piranha's nest, or when piranha are unintentionally caught and handled by fishermen.

I was therefore advised to net the piranha, avoid handling and transfer them to their new tank. The tank in which they were housed was devoid of rocks or plants, with no hiding places. I was confident I could catch them in record time. Manoeuvring the net under water towards the fish, I swiftly scooped it out of the water, convinced it contained a piranha. But on inspection, the net was empty. I repeated this numerous times, targeting different individuals, while noticing the aquarium keepers were smirking. Finally one enquired.

"Do you think you've got the right net for the job there Bill?" On examining the net, there was a large slit along the seam, where the first piranha had effortlessly sliced through the material providing an escape route for himself and his colleagues.

Giving injections to birds and animals, is a job that all zoo personnel have to do from time to time. While humans usually stand submissively, roll up their shirt sleeves, then feint. Animals and birds prefer to play catch me if you can.

The rhea is a large flightless South American bird, the same size as an emu. And a smaller version of its cousin the ostrich and is sometimes referred to as the South American ostrich.

Zoos usually provide rheas with spacious paddocks in which to roam. This is ideal until you have to catch one. With their long legs and muscular thighs they are natural sprinters. Not as fast as an ostrich. The world's fastest running bird has been clocked at 45 mph. But rheas can effortlessly reach speeds of 35mph and they are more agile. They can side step and body swerve, to football premiership standard. Swiftly changing direction, using their large wings like sails. They can also swim, which they readily do to escape enemies.

I had to administer an injection of an anti-inflammatory drug to a male rhea, who had arthritis in one of his feet. This caused him to limp slightly when walking, but didn't affect his running ability. One attempt had already been made to catch him. The rhea raced around the paddock at high speed, while another keeper and I followed at an ever-decreasing speed. We left the paddock, breathlessly informing the assembled spectators, we had completed the daily task of exercising the bird.

I invited suggestions from the other keepers, on how we could catch the rhea and administer an injection. There is always one in every team and his suggestion:

"Why don't you give it an injection to slow it down?"

Another suggestion was to imitate the South American cowboys of the pampas plains, who hunt animals including rheas, using bolas. These are short ropes with wooden balls attached. The cowboys skilfully throw the bolas from galloping horses. They wrap around a rhea's legs, bringing it to the ground. I decided against becoming a cowboy, after envisaging my head encased in blood soaked wooden balls.

I decided instead to enlist the athletic skills of Stephen, a young elephant keeper, who hailed from the parts of Scotland where the roads are almost vertical. Stephen had lost the ability to walk at a very early age and had ran everywhere ever since.

It was rumoured, he cycled the ten mile round daily trip from his home to the zoo. I didn't believe this for a minute. I suspect he ran alongside his bike.

We had a plan. As soon as Stephen apprehended the rhea, I would assist him in restraining it. Stephen vaulted over the fence of the rhea paddock. The rhea ran, but Stephen ran faster, running alongside it and giving me the thumbs up, before overtaking it and punching the air. This went on for several laps, till I hauled him in for a pit stop.

"Stephen, this is not the Scotland versus South America all species marathon. We need to catch the bird. Just grab a wing, hang on and I'll join you and grab the other wing."

Stephen shot off again, catching up to the rhea with ease and grabbing the end of a wing.

As the duo turned the circuit and appeared to be hand in hand, I leapt and grabbed the rhea's other wing. Despite having a human hanging on both wings, it didn't slow the rhea down. We applied foot brakes, digging our heels in, to no avail. And had no alternative other than to participate in the little known sport of rhea skiing.

We hung on for a lap and half, each still clutching a wing. But other than make a wish, we were unsure of what to do next. As the rhea accelerated, we were dragged through the dust, like the cowboys who halted stagecoaches by diving in amongst the horses. (This was prior to the health and safety directive, when communication chords were installed on all stagecoaches)

After the rhea was satisfied that he had covered us with sufficient dust, he slowed down to a canter, then a slow trot. Finally he parked, leaning against the fence.

Having two dust covered zoo men attached to his wings, must have tired him to some degree, because his knees buckled and he sat down. Stephen and I breathing heavily, sat either side of him. We had him in our grasp, if only we could summon enough strength to do the grasping. Too late! He was up and off around the paddock again. Time for plan B. In the zoo office at the other end of the zoo, I had some hollow rheas eggs.

I always kept a stock of these, as they are highly prized by hobbyists who decorate and paint eggs. Egg-sperts I think they are called.

I asked Stephen to run to the zoo office and collect two of the primrose coloured eggs. I opened the gate of the rhea paddock and he shot off like a roadrunner on drugs. As I was about to close the gate, he reappeared with the eggs! (I told you he was fast.) The eggs were then placed in a prominent position in the paddock.

Male rheas are doting fathers. Not only do they care for their mate's eggs, they care for other female's eggs too. The eggs, which the females drop anywhere and everywhere, are manoeuvred by the males into small craters they excavate.

Sometimes up to sixty eggs are in a clutch. But not all of these hatch. The ones on the perimeter of the clutch are visible and not incubated. But they serve a purpose. They are sacrificed to predators, while the male safeguards and incubates a smaller number of eggs. Eventually rearing around a dozen youngsters.

The male rhea lost no time in making a bee-line for the eggs, giving them a brief inspection tap with his beak, before promptly folding his legs and squatting on them. We allowed him to get comfortable before making a move. He drooped his wings and half closed his eyes, as maternal feelings came over him. I quickly sat astride his back. In this position, his legs folded out of action, he was prevented from rising. Stephen brought the needle and a pair of scissors and swapped places with me. I cut away a small patch of feathers to avoid contamination. Inserting the needle, I administered the long overdue injection. We had to perform this task twice a week for six weeks. So I anticipated at least one cardiac arrest by the end of the month. As we released the bird, a young boy among the crowd of onlookers was questioning his father about the proceedings

"Dad, why was the zoo keeper cutting off the bird's feathers?"

The father raised his voice, enabling the maximum amount of people to hear this gem of knowledge.

"Well you see son, the birds have to be caught from time to time and have their wings clipped, or they would just fly away."

COCKATOO'D AT THE CATHEDRAL

Even before Hereward worked at the zoo he was assaulted by a zoo inmate. During his interview, a stuffed grizzly bear toppled over pinning him to the floor. The zoo manager separated the pair and informed the nervous lad,

"Animals seem attracted to you. You've got the job."

Hereward should have taken the bear attack as an omen. His first day at the Australian zoo would be memorable for the multiple attacks he would sustain.

A daily task on the bird section was to clean the large zoo aviary nick named Cockatoo Cathedral. So called, because the huge old Victorian aviary had a high ornate roof. The Cathedral was home to over almost a hundred mainly ex-pet sulphur crested cockatoos. These beautiful snowy white birds with lemon crests and engaging personalities, used to be regularly sold in Australian pet shops. But the highly social and intelligent birds require specialist care. When this is denied, frustrated, they incessantly scream and the volume of a cockatoo's screams usually contributes to them being swiftly re-homed. Most of the cathedral's cockatoos had learned to speak and mimic sounds, especially tunes and songs. Others preferred uttering swear words and curses. It was like being in the midst of a football crowd. The majority conducted a sing a long or chanted inoffensive slogans, while a hard core group of belligerent yobs turned the air blue.

When cleaning the cathedral you had to be on your guard. Tame cockatoos with a grudge are often the most treacherous. Their ploy was to speak sweetly, approach bowing their head, extending their crest, inviting you to stroke them.

45

It was unwise to oblige, as they would often then launch an attack.

This would greatly excite their colleagues, who screamed, wings extended crests raised. Sometimes the group mentality would kick in and the whole flock would take to the wing, screeching and frenziedly circling the keeper.

Many a bird keeper under siege in the cockatoo cathedral has been heard yelling at the top of his voice:

"Help! the flocking cockatoos are on the attack." Or words to that effect. Sweeping the Cathedral floor was arduous. Using a long headed broom, by time you had swept a small area, you had ten or more cockatoos hitching a ride, singing whistling or cursing. Then one or more would decide to ascend the broom handle homing in on your fingers

If you wore shoes, laces would inevitably be picked undone. To evade this keepers always appeared to be performing a tap dance. If you wore Wellingtons the birds would see it as a challenge to perforate them. Or alight on your trousers and poke their heads inside the dark interiors, sometimes disappearing inside. There they would either chew your socks, or get lodged, squawking incessantly until they were pulled out. Even your zoo keeper's peaked cap, which afforded some protection from head banging individuals, would soon have cockatoos locked on to the peak with their beaks. Wings closed, lifelessly swinging back and forth, like oversized corks on a bushman's hat.

Being assaulted was bad enough, but made worse when gawping zoo visitors congregated encouraging other visitors to do likewise:

"Just have a look at what this guy has trained these parrots to do."

In order to brave the cockatoo gauntlet, it was imperative to complete the cleaning quickly, then make a swift exit. Teaching Hereward the cathedral cleaning routine would be challenging.

He was incredibly slow and always seemed half asleep prompting many a keeper to voice the catch phrase:

"Is Hereward awake?"

As we tap danced in unison. I impressed upon Hereward not to loiter. But Hereward was so slow, he would make a sloth look hyperactive. Even when harassed his top speed was equivalent to that of a resident at Madame Tussauds. He had also obviously never used a broom, not unusual among trainees, who often assumed brooms moved automatically and didn't require being pushed.

Within no time Hereward was cloaked in a slow moving scrum of cockatoos.

As the morning morphed into afternoon and Hereward had finally finished sweeping the Cathedral floor, I was exhausted from the marathon tap dancing session and the floor needed to be swept again. Somewhere in the quivering white feathered pyramid, was a rookie bird keeper, on his first day, in his first aviary and by the sound of laboured breathing, uttering his last breaths.

I desperately pulled screeching cockatoos off Hereward, to allow him to at least breath. Then dragged him gasping for air towards the aviary door. He was covered in cuts and scratches and snowy down feathers. He looked like he'd done a shift at a flour mill, having collected a covering of white dust from the cockatoo's powder down feathers. These are feathers that produce something similar to talcum powder that assist preening.

'Smothered by cockatoos on his first day at the zoo,' does not look good on the tombstone. But Hereward had survived, just and credit was due.

"You did well Hereward. It's simply because they are so tame, these cockatoos are such a nightmare."

Hereward, white-faced and spitting feathers, shook his head in disbelief.

"If they're tame! I'd hate to be waylaid by a flock of wild ones"

COUNTING BEARS

Some people have a desire to work with animals, but don't have the right disposition. Being tense or nervous around animals has a negative effect. Animals intuitively interpret body language.

To them, sudden movements, frequent eye contact and other nervous behaviour, is indistinguishable from aggressive behaviour. It's no surprise, that these individuals are more likely to be bitten or attacked.

A nervous young keeper nicknamed Shakin Stephen, had joined the zoo keeping staff. His mother thought it was the ideal job, which would help her son overcome his fear of animals. This was unlikely. Stephen permanently lived in fear of being bitten, stung, pecked, or nibbled to death by a non-human. And he was constantly looking over his shoulder in anticipation of this taking place. Even when small birds flew overhead he ducked.

On his first week at the zoo, Stephen was recruited to work on the bear section. Where the first morning task, was the cleaning of the outdoor bear enclosures.

The bears as usual, would be safely shut away in the inside quarters. To tempt them inside, loaves hollowed out and filled with honey, malt, or peanut butter were on offer. The bears absolutely loved this breakfast, but bears also love to sleep. To awaken any sleeping bears who missed the breakfast bell, keepers yelled, banged metal buckets and dishes, making as much row as they could. This normally worked. Any dozing bear would be awoken, stagger out of its sleeping place, scratching and yawning ready for breakfast. Once the bears were all confined in the inside quarters, a head count was undertaken. This sounded easier than it was. In the dimly lit area, the bears would be milling about and it was easy to count one bear twice.

Each keeper did their own count and only when every keeper's count tallied, were the large sliding metal gates to the bear pit opened and the cleaning crew sent in.

This particular morning, the head keeper of bears was leaning over the wall of the public walkway above the bear pit, watching the cleaning crew.

"I don't want to alarm you, but we seem to be a bear short. Its Bruno. You know where he'll be. Try not to wake him. He's like a bear with a sore head in the morning."

The head keeper suppressed a giggle. There was no missing bear. And all the keepers apart from Stephen knew it. This was a regular wind up by the head keeper, when a 'green horn' was on bear pit cleaning detail.

Stephen on hearing this was like a coiled spring and entrusted with the wheelbarrow, went into Lewis Hamilton mode. Racing around the enclosure at top speed, negotiating the rocky outcrops and large logs that were too heavy to move, but which the bears effortlessly rolled around. Stephen had a dependency on peppermints. When nervous, he stuffed these in his mouth at an ever-increasing rate, till he resembled a well-fed hamster. The cleaning operation had been completed in record time. Stephen was now racing towards the exit, his long legs almost a blur. While his colleagues followed at a more leisurely pace.

As Stephen rounded the last corner, he came face to face with the dark furry form of the eight-foot high bear. Paws raised, mouth wide open, ready for a big hug.

The bear pit was home to Kodiak bears, the island race that together with the polar bear are the largest bear species. Standing upright Kodiaks can reach over 3 metres and weigh half a ton. In a confrontation all bears are bad news. They can out run, out climb and out swim humans. If you play hide and seek with them, (not advisable), their excellent sense of smell will locate you in no time. The best advice is to play dead and don't pray too loudly.

Stephen played faint so convincingly he really fainted, spitting out peppermints like a machine gun before performing a full frontal dive into a barrow full of bear manure.

The bear incident confirmed what everybody knew, including Stephen. He wasn't cut out to be a zoo keeper and without persuasion handed in his notice.

Stephen is probably convinced to this day, he had escaped the clutches of the bear due to the bravery of his colleagues and was indebted to them for saving his life. They never had the heart to tell him, Bruno, the carnivore he had encountered, was a twenty-year-old resident of a zoo social club, a moth eaten bear rug propped up on two broom handles.

BOXING CLEVER

Transferring animals from one zoo to another involves a lot of planning.

Each species and each individual, react differently to being confined in a travel crate. They may be anxious. Some have to be slightly sedated to prevent panicking. While others take a zoo transfer in their stride. Giraffes have often been transported by road, in roofless trailer crates with their heads and necks exposed.

Hyperactive animals like monkeys are surprisingly quiet on the road and seem to enjoy the journey. Tigers, lions and other big cats, can be fed in open travel crates prior to a move. This accustoms them to the travel accommodation, which they usually adapt to without incident. Crates are never ultra spacious, this prevents the animals hurting themselves if they do panic and in the case of large animals damaging the crate and escaping.

Smaller birds are usually transported in cages. But on long distances the cages are often placed inside latticed crates. In these dimly lit surroundings, birds will remain more at ease and less stressed, than if they could be viewed from all sides in cages.

A cassowary is a large flightless bird from Australia and New Guinea. Notoriously known, as the bird that can kill with one kick. This is not exaggeration, people have been killed and zoo keepers seriously injured by cassowaries. They are solitary by nature, but are so bad tempered, even when being paired up for breeding, will often rather fight than mate. Their method of attack is to jump and launch a series of drop kicks. This can be devastating to anyone or anything on the receiving end, as the inner toe on each cassowary's foot is shaped like a dagger. With their reputation, cassowaries in zoos are treated with utmost caution. When keepers enter their enclosure they often carry wooden shields for protection.

One night in 1952, Sydney Police found Robert Cook lying in a city street. He had over thirty puncture wounds to his legs, stomach, chest and face, He was lucky to be alive. But his attackers weren't human. Foolishly after dark, he had entered the cassowary enclosure at Taronga zoo, planning to steal eggs. But he didn't expect the egg's owners to be so violently opposed to his plan.

A bad tempered cassowary called Cassius, was being transferred to a new zoo. A travel crate had to be constructed, strong enough to withstand any kicks Cassius might deliver. Jed the zoo carpenter was old school, who built items made to last. Following the specifications, the travel crate he built resembled an item of oak furniture. So heavy and bulky, we could only have crated Cassius if he had been lured into it in Jed's workshop.

A new lighter crate was positioned at the entrance to the cassowary enclosure. The crate had a heavy door and enough catches locks and bolts to contain Houdini. The door was held open at the ready. All that was required was for Cassius to be herded inside. Simple! Not really.

Cassowaries are unpredictable to say the least. You can restrain an ostrich, by putting a small hood over their head and ostrich 'hoods' have been specially made for this task for centuries. Try hooding a cassowary and you will be launched into orbit by a bird with more kicking power than the Brazilian football team.

Keepers took on the role of sheepdogs, attempting to herd Cassius into his travel crate. But every time Cassius got near the crate, he body swerved and jogged around the paddock dispersing the keepers. After demonstrating that the keepers were more like sheep than sheepdogs. Cassius did several laps of honour, steadily gaining speed, before shooting inside the crate like an athlete high on a banned substance.

The door was swiftly closed, with all available zoo keepers putting their weight against it, while securing all locks, catches and bolts. Unfortunately this did nothing to contain Cassius. When he entered the crate at speed, he was just passing through. Kicking out the rear panel of the crate, he sprinted off round the zoo scattering zoo visitors in his wake.

When opening travel crates, the animals have to be restrained promptly to prevent escape. A common saying among zoo keepers when handling or catching animals, is he who hesitates gets bitten. One young bird keeper called William, had a nose that veered slightly to the left. The result of a failed attempt to remove a Great Indian Hornbill from its travel crate. With a wingspan of over five feet, this tropical Asiatic species, is the largest flying fruit eating bird. Their flamboyant plumage, expressive eyes, long eyelashes and playful extrovert nature, makes them popular zoo birds. But despite possessing what looks like a formidable beak and a call that sounds more like a guard dog than a bird, they are usually unaggressive birds.

Hornbills have similar beaks to the South American Toucans, but the two bird families are unrelated. They feed on similar foods, mainly forest fruits and berries.

Hornbills have a unique security system for protecting their nest. The female is sealed in the tree cavity by the male, using mud that hardens like concrete. Leaving just a small gap, through which the male feeds her. She remains imprisoned in this maternity chamber, till after her eggs have hatched and her youngsters are ready to fly.

On the day of William's encounter with the Hornbill, a large bird crate was carried into the bird room and the lid removed. Crouching in one corner on a bed of straw, was a seemingly passive male Great Indian Hornbill. William eager to impress his colleagues, took the initiative. But instead of quickly grabbing the bird's beak, while it was disorientated and dazzled by the lights in the room. He leaned down into the crate and hesitated, giving the Hornbill time to shoot out its long neck and even longer bill, expertly seizing the most prominent part of William's anatomy, his nose.

Hornbills are adept as manipulating very small items with their beak, or in William's case, gripping them in a vice like hold.

In captivity they will expertly catch grapes and other food items that are thrown to them. Young tame hornbills will even play with a ball, bouncing and skilfully catching it.

This ability to catch moving items in the air, is the basis of a predatory habit, that was not generally known when hornbills were first housed in aviaries with smaller birds.

Being fruit eaters, it was assumed smaller aviary companions were safe. Until hornbills were observed in communal aviaries. Perched in a prominent position they would nonchalantly catch small birds as they flew past, quickly gulping them down. Despite William's nose being above average length and girth, it would always come off second in a jousting contest with a large hornbill. A terrier with a rat, was the phrase that came to mind.

As William's head was shaken violently from side to side, reminiscent of an enthusiastic heavy metal fan, he gripped the sides of the travel crate and moaned. His colleagues tried to prise open the Hornbill's beak, prompting the bird to growl like a junkyard dog and tighten its grip, while William's eyes filled with tears. One keeper unsure what to do, pulled on William's head, which only brought more tears to the head's owner. Finally the hornbill voluntarily released its grip.

The hornbill legacy would haunt William throughout his zoo career. Much to his irritation, newcomers to the bird section never failed to enquire, "So William, why the nickname Horn Bill?"

Sometimes animal crates arrived at a zoo with no paperwork and when opened up revealed a few surprises. This was the case when a large crate labelled 'Sunbirds' was delivered via forklift truck, through the double doors of the Bird House at Chester Zoo almost filling the room.

The bird keepers scratched their heads in bewilderment. Large crates usually contained smaller crates or cages, keeping the birds quiet and insulated during stopovers at airport terminals. But this was the largest single bird crate any of the bird staff had ever encountered. The head keeper Jim chewed on his pipe while circumnavigating the shed size object.

"They must be buying birds in bulk now. Or somebody's taken advantage of a special offer, buy an ostrich and get one free. Well what you waiting for? Let's see what's inside."

A keeper was about to lever open the lid with a crowbar, when the crate moved sideways a good ten inches. The keeper looked at it in bemusement,

"Maybe they all decided to fly in one direction at the same time." When the keeper finally opened the tightly nailed lid, a large black paw appeared immediately in the gap. In an emergency there is no substitute for experience. So we all jumped behind the head keeper. One apprentice keeper notoriously short sighted, remained staring at the paw, which was slowly lifting the lid of the crate.

"Relax guys, I can clearly see five bird's beaks."

The head keeper pulled him back by his collar.

"They're not beaks lad, they're claws!"

Realising what he had just said. The head keeper spat his pipe out and shot through the open door like Seb Coe. Meanwhile, his keepers, a mass of writhing arms and legs, were simultaneously trying to exit through the three-foot wide door frame.

Closer inspection revealed, the writing on the crate's faded label read, 'Sun bears,' not 'Sunbirds.' The occupants, two Malayan sun bears, are not the largest of bears, but they possess five inch long claws and are capable of inflicting a more memorable bite than a sunbird.

In my effort to limit my carbon footprint to the size of a bee hummingbird's egg I refuse to drive. The truth is, I have tried, but failed to learn under generations of instructors. My excuse for being a non-driver, is that I'm waiting for more instructors to be trained up.

My aversion to driving, was triggered by traumatic experiences as a youth in a notorious 'zoo van.' A vehicle long past its scrap date, which qualified as a van purely because it had 'zoo van,' printed on the side.

Essentially a two-man vehicle, Old Harry the driver, who had learned to drive in the army, probably under the Duke of Wellington, required a second man to hold the rear doors closed. With the cab sealed from the van's interior, the door holder was in semi-darkness. For the entire journey you were thrown about the rusty interior, colliding with animal crates, nets and other paraphernalia. On being released you went into crab-mode. Bent double, for at least an hour you could only walk sideways.

On one particular trip with Harry, we had to collect two peacocks and a pair of Barnacle Geese, from a waterfowl breeder who lived less than twenty miles from the zoo. Predictably we got lost, as Harry tried one of his short cuts, which always turned out to be a short cut to a previous destination. After visiting various English counties, as usual Harry got hungry. Nauseous from van imprisonment, I loitered in a teashop, while Harry devoured a stack of cakes that blocked out light from the window.

"Those Biblical Geese will be wondering where we've got to Bill."

"They will Harry. I just hope we can find this place soon, as Biblical Geese are not particularly long lived birds."

With the sun descending and Harry moaning he was hungry again, I asked directions at a farmhouse we had passed several times already. This turned out to be the address we had been searching for all along. (Which explained why a couple on the driveway of the house, waved excitedly every time we passed by.)

Harry had thoughtfully only brought one bird crate. After the honking Barnacle Geese were crated up, Harry thrust a peacock under each of my arms, instructing me to grip their legs and insisted they wouldn't mind riding in the back with me. Inexperienced and unaware that Harry knew as much about birds as he did about navigation, I at first agreed.

"But how do I hold the doors Harry?"

"Could you in some way grip them with your feet?"

"Harry I'm not a circus performer, the first bump in the road we hit, due to this vehicle's lack of suspension, I'll shoot out like a human torpedo accompanied by two peacocks. Any other ideas?"

"Tell you what Bill, just hold the doors shut as you usually do. Don't worry about the peacocks, they'll be okay just wandering about. Meanwhile, why don't you have a kip, you look shattered?"

With two deafening bangs Harry imprisoned me once more in the van's dark interior. Deafened by the echoes of the honking Geese, the situation didn't improve as the peacocks decided to spar.

Aware that their pristine feathers are easily damaged. Peacock sparring usually involves a lot of wing slapping and air kicking, with minimum physical contact. Usually ending with the dominant bird chasing the loser away. But with no exit route for the loser, the fight got very physical and went the distance. Occasionally a wing slap or kick, would miss the opponent and hit me. All I could do was hang on to the doors and spit feathers. On my release from the van, I looked like I had been in a psychedelic pillow fight.

Harry's zoo van driving career finally reached the terminus. The rear doors were repaired and Harry rode alone, without a navigator. This didn't perturb Harry. Even though his sense of direction was nil. Harry reasoned, because the world was round, if he kept driving, he would eventually reach his destination.

Receiving instructions to deliver a pair of Griffon vultures, Harry headed north before pulling into a transport cafe. On entering the cafe, a pair of unsavoury guys rudely pushed passed him and briskly walked out. After finishing his coffee and trademark stack of sandwiches, Harry went to check the van. On opening the doors he was shocked to see there were no vultures. Harry was convinced, the guys he'd just seen had taken them.

When in doubt Harry always called his 'knowledgeable' brother.

"Geoff, I've just had a pair of vultures stolen from out of the van while I was in the transport caff,"

"I'm not surprised, vulture laundering is on the rise. They steal birds to order and send them over to the continent. Then they dye them a different colour."

"I bet that's the plan. So they can't be identified "

It seemed lost on Harry, no matter what colour they were dyed, a pair of four-foot high vultures with a six foot wingspan, would still be easily identified.

Finally Harry rang the zoo.

"Where the hell are you Harry?"

"Manchester, five minutes away from Bellevue Zoo. I'm a victim of vulture launderers. I put up a fight, but there were two of em, big blokes. Then there was a high speed car chase through red lights. But they got away. The vultures are probably over in Belgium by now being sprayed. It's a job for Interpol."

"Harry, the vultures are sitting in their crate."

"But the crate is not in my van. That's the problem."

"I know."

"How do you know?"

"Because the vultures are here. Don't you ever read your paperwork Harry? They were waiting to be loaded into your van before you sped off this morning.

And you're not supposed to be taking them to Bellevue Zoo. You're supposed be taking them to Chessington Zoo Surrey, just down the road."

"Phew...It's a good thing I didn't pick em up then."

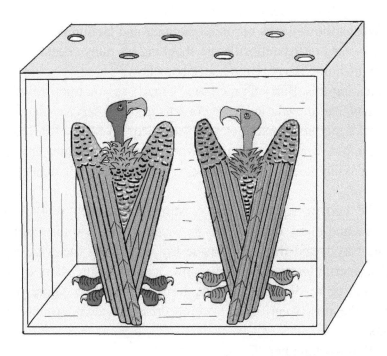

SWANEE, HOW I LOVE YOU

I wasn't in the best mood, one of my bird keepers was on holiday the other, a malingerer / hypochondriac, not only decided to call in sick, but also wanted to discuss his health issues.

"I've got a fever and my hand's swollen up again from when I was savaged by that lovebird. If you really want me to, I'll come in. But I'm in bad shape. I can't see me being much help."

What followed was chronic coughing and laboured breathing so bad I swear I heard defibrillators shocking his puny chest.

"Stay home Barry, I'll manage somehow."

Hearing this, Barry chirped up. "Great! see you tomorrow."

I now had the whole bird section to feed and service on my own. To make matters worse, our van was in for an MOT. My transport was the oldest exhibit from the wheel barrow museum, prompting every passing keeper to comment, "At least it's better than walking Bill."

The barrow squeaked like a strangled screech owl. Alerting pigeons and every other flying free loader a mobile bird table was on its way round the zoo. I made my way along the winding zoo paths, intermittently doing my Tippi Hendren impression, of manic arm waving to disperse flocking birds. Suddenly a figure jumped out of the mist wearing a flowered dressing gown, sombrero and tights

"You working here?"

Why would he assume this? Possibly the zoo uniform, cap and wheel barrow laden with buckets of bird food was a clue."

"How can I help?"

The guy thumped his chest like a gorilla who had just got a

parking ticket.

"I have overwhelming need to watch swans mating. You may help?"

I was about to escort this visitor to the exit by the scruff of his neck but suddenly the guy pirouetted on the spot and disappeared from sight, before jumping high evidently from a crouched position.

Extending a limp wrist he shook my hand and bowed his head before announcing.

"Beckeroff."

I looked him up and down. "Did you just tell me to?"

"I am Alexis Beckeroff, dancer. Performing Swan Lake at the Palace Theatre." I need to see swans making lovey dovey, so that I can relate to my ballerina on stage."

Recently the zoo boss had impressed on us the importance of being visitor friendly, which I suppose included passifying nutters.

"You want to observe swans, let's see."

"You want bribe, it's the same everywhere these days, so what's the going rate to watch pair of swans mating?"

"As it so happens, we have a pair of Australian Black Swans who are ready to nest at the main waterfowl pond. Black Swans."

"I preferring white, what other colours have you got them in?"

"None. You don't get many white species of swans in captivity, they are too aggressive."

Alexis danced as he accompanied me to the large waterfowl pond, performing pirouettes and pausing at intervals to do knee's bend exercises.

When we arrived at the pond the Black Swans were swimming amid a group of ducks.

"There you are, that's the Black Swans on the water."

"Ahh! and they have so many babies already."

"They're ducks. This is a waterfowl pond."

"Don't the watering fowl mind all the ducks and swans sharing their pond?"

"The swans and ducks are the watering fowl."

"Okay, please command the swans to mate over here"

"I can't do that, they'll mate in the water."

"Underwater? There will just be bubbles. I can't perform bubbles."

"They mate <u>on</u> the water, like most waterfowl. Look! The male swan is swimming around the female, she's wagging her tail, you might just be in luck."

Facing each other, the swans indulged in the ritual of head dipping while emitting their piping calls. This was followed by 'necking,' the male laying his neck across the lowered neck of the female. The female sank lower in the water inviting the male to mount her, which he did, almost completely submerging his mate. Task completed, after less than a minute of romance he was swimming alongside her again.

"And that's that."

"That was what?"

"They mated."

"I don't want speed dating. Whammy bammy, thank you Swanee. I want to see romantic seduction and a whirlwind of passion." Alexis started spinning on the spot.

" Do you think you could you go easy on the pirouettes mate ? You're making me dizzy.

"I demand refunding."

"You never paid any money."

"If I had, I would be demand full refunding. You have denied me inspiration. How can I explain in English without being hurtful? You are, useless idiot. But it's been pleasure." In full view of a group of keepers Alex grabbed both my shoulders, planting sloppy kisses on both my cheeks. Before bounding off up a zoo path probably to see if any other zoo animals were mating.

A keeper approached.

"You've met Mad Max then."

"You mean Alexis the ballet dancer."

"Is that who he is today? Last month we had him jumping up naked out of litter bins, claiming he was a space rocket."

MIND THE DOORS

When running a small zoo or bird garden its essential to have some practical skills.

Yet some zoo owners I've come across were woefully devoid of these. Finding just one lonely spanner in an ancient tool chest, I asked one zoo boss where he kept tools to tackle aviary repairs. He replied, "The hammer we did have, belonged to a guy who left."

In my time in zoos and bird gardens I've often had to take on the tasks better suited to a horticulturist, electrician or bricklayer. Consequently plants died, walls fell down and lights went out. Aviaries that are badly constructed, often prove to be hazardous and a nightmare to service. I was advised by one zoo boss, "Never ever slam the finch aviary door." A simple request, but under the circumstances difficult to comply with. The reinforced door on a metal frame, previously part of a chimp enclosure, (or it could have been a bank vault), was fitted with two large suspension springs from a heavy goods vehicle. The door operated like a giant mousetrap. One morning I found out why slamming the door was inadvisable. As it was closing, despite hanging on for dear life, embracing it like you would a rich uncle. It slammed shut and simultaneously all the perches and nest boxes in the aviary fell down. The simple task of securing perches and nest boxes had been ignored. Instead all effort was put into trying to prevent the heavy spring loaded door from slamming shut. Badly constructed aviaries and enclosures require more maintenance, as they are regularly being patched up, but never to a satisfactory standard and there is more chance of inmates escaping.

As the sun rose on my first morning at one zoo, on opening the curtains, I saw a large guy bent double, working away in the walled kitchen garden. I mentioned this later to the zoo owner.

"That would be Malcolm, he's no gardener though. He's Mavis's mate. Mavis and Malcolm are black bears."

Apparently the furry duo regularly climbed through the flimsy roof of their ramshackle enclosure and over the adjacent wall into the kitchen garden. Here they spent so much time 'gardening,' their food was placed in nearby greenhouses for them. At one bird garden most of the aviaries housed white mice. Bred for feeding to the carnivorous birds such as owls, hawks etc. They had escaped, or more accurately walked in a procession out of the perforated wooden cages which were their temporary homes.

The mice were very popular with the public, who would usually make the observation when viewing the aviaries: "Aren't those mice sweet? Oh look! And there's some birds in there too." Sometimes there were horrified complaints, when the public witnessed owls and even pheasants catching live mice and nonchalantly swallowing them down whole. Within time the albino mice integrated into the community. Having hybridised with the resident house mouse population, they were no longer a whiter shade of pale.

Struggling with two food buckets on my initial food run at the above bird garden, I entered the first aviary and crouched in the small safety porch, obviously designed for one of Snow White's helpers. Although safety porches can prevent escapes. It's often assumed birds always make a sudden rush to the aviary door as soon as it's opened, which is not the case. Birds soon accustom themselves to the perimeters of their aviary and even if they do escape often try to get back inside. Embracing two food buckets inside the aviary porch, I tried to enter the aviary by pushing against the second door, until I realised it opened outwards. This meant it was impossible to open unless I reversed halfway out of the safety porch. Then leaning forward, holding open the door into the aviary, head bowed and knees bent. I had to leap, frog-like, into aviary.

Fortunately I was propelled to my destination, by the outer door clouting me on the backside. To my despair I discovered all the aviaries had identical safety porches. This increased the chances of birds escaping when both doors were held open.

The opposite of what a safety porch was supposed to prevent.

When I pointed this out to the eccentric bird garden owner, logic packed up, got on its bike and went home.

"You just need to practise going in and out a bit more. The safety porches are small because during construction I ran out of wire. But little Jenny did your job for ages. She managed."

He looked me up and down.

"If you lost a few pounds you'd shoot through those aviaries like a whippet."

"With respect, it's very difficult due to the design of safety porches for anything to shoot through. Even a whippet"

"But that's the whole idea! Any aviary-ologist (aviculturist was the word that eluded him) will tell you. If it's difficult to get in, it is doubly difficult for the birds to get out.

That's why we have safety porches in all the aviaries. Without a safety porch, when you entered the aviary, not only would the birds escape, you'd let all the mice out."

IN THE HOT SEAT
AT THE ZOO CALL CENTRE

Zoos now have staff to deal with telephone enquiries.

But in days gone by, the zoo telephone was regarded with dread by zookeepers, as it was their responsibility to deal with enquiries from the general public. Most of these were sensible and reasonable.

Then there were the others.

"Can you settle an argument, is the flamingo a dance or a bird?"

On April 1st every year, the same predictable calls came through.

"Can I speak to a Miss Ele Phant or a Mr G Raffe?"

Other calls start off normal, you are sucked in and then the loony tune starts to play.

"We are thinking of getting a parrot, never had one before, what type do you suggest?" My mind's eye scans the species suitable for the novice. Budgerigars, Lovebirds, Cockatiels.

"Myself I don't care what sort we have, but it's causing a family rift. The twins are Manchester United supporters, so obviously they want a red and white one, definitely no blue. But the wife insists on apricot, as she's just had the kitchen done out in puce."

"Well I would suggest you contact a reputable bird dealer who will send you a colour chart."

David Attenborough has a lot to answer for. The morning after the screening of one of his popular wildlife documentaries, there was always phone calls enquiring about animals who featured in the programme.

"Where can we purchase some Penguins? I was thinking of having a small flock in the outdoor swimming pool, during the winter when it's not in use. It would be great to watch them performing. Diving through hoops and chasing balls, doing all their usual tricks, the kids would love it."

"Penguins doing tricks! Are you sure you're not thinking of dolphins?"

"Dolphins! Well I suppose we could have some of them too, a mixture."

Some people are inspired to acquire a pet, after seeing it depicted as a cartoon character.

"Help me out here. I've been all through the yellow pages. Where can I get a roadrunner? Kids won't be happy till they get one. They are out on their bikes all day, so it would get enough exercise. We do have a cat and she's a hunter, but I'm sure she won't keep up with old R and R when he puts his foot down."

Enquiries seeking advice on animals acquired as pets, often begs the question, why didn't the owner do some research prior to obtaining the pet?

"Okay, so I bought this baby owl, which you now tell me is a full grown Little Owl. We've had him six months. He's feeding and not shy anymore. But he's such a disappointment."

"In what way?"

"Well I thought he would at least be saying a few words by now."

Zoos are frequently offered unwanted pets. But there is limited space in zoo collections. Still people often assume they are doing you a favour by donating their pet and it doesn't always register when you decline their offer.

"Following a family meeting, we decided our turkey flock would be much happier living at your zoo."

I wish I could have been at the meeting, then I could have informed the family we have no room for turkeys. But I would have been wasting my time, the family spokesman wasn't a listener.

"They are all tame apart from Derek, the oldest stag (why the term for a male turkey is the same as that for a male deer, I will never fathom)

"We can't take turkeys I'm afraid."

"My wife has found the best way to deal with Derek's attacks, is to wear dustbin lids strapped to her legs as shields and it seems to work."

This guy not only wanted us to re-home his flock of turkeys, he was advising we dress like musicians in a one man band.

"We can't take any turkeys. We have no room for them."

He pointed over my head.

"You've got turkeys over there. Near the pheasants."

He was pointing to a group of Francolins. Partridge-like game birds, from Asia and Africa.

"The birds you are referring to are Francolins."

"So what's the problem? Put our turkeys with Francolin's turkeys."

"This is the situation. We can't take your turkeys under any circumstances. Not one turkey, not even a turkey portion, now or in the future."

The guy looked at me quizzically.

"Let me get this right, you're saying you can't take our turkeys."

I nodded like a toy dog in the back of a speeding car.

"Well I have been grossly misled."

"In what way?"

"You've no signs or other information regarding being unable to take turkeys. Consequently, I've turned up here in good faith with a car full of turkeys."

A forefinger prodded my forehead.

" Do you know what you are? You're a time waster."

Zoos run on tight budgets and when valuable exotic species are offered free of charge, it can seem too good to be true. Sometimes it is. And a sultry sexy voice that is ultra complimentary, should always be treated with suspicion. A lady with obvious feminine charms accosted me.

"You've been highly recommended to me. I'm in desperate need of assistance and advice from an expert like yourself."

(Alarm bells should ring at this stage, but you soak up the

flattery and throw caution over your shoulder.)

"I'm here to help. I only hope I can be of some assistance"

"I have a pair of breeding blue and gold macaws. I don't have time to look after them and I'm taking their aviary down. There are also a few budgies etc. It's a large aviary which is fairly new. You are most welcome to it, if you agree to re-home the occupants?"

Macaws are expensive and a great attraction, I immediately agreed, salivating at the opportunity of acquiring a pair of these charismatic birds and an aviary to house them, all completely free.

It all seemed straightforward. Until the lady arrived with almost twenty pet carriers.

She then rattled off a list of celebrity names:

"Madonna, Kylie, Lady Gaga, Ant and Dec."

While opening the carriers to reveal 15 guinea pigs, five chickens, a lop eared rabbit, two obese budgies. Long John, a one legged Herring gull, with the biting ability to rival a Jack Russell and Speedo the tortoise who had his name emblazoned across his shell.

When I steadfastly refused to take this menagerie, she reminded me, I had given my word I would re-home the occupants of her aviary.

I dug my heels in. The local authority ran the zoo and menagerie lady was now threatening to complain to her friends, the mayor and prominent councillors.

Hoping for support, I contacted my boss. Who at first backed me. Then when he heard about the mayor, backed me into a corner. Instructing me to swiftly award permanent zoo residency, to Speedo and co.

Herding up the Guinea Pigs assisted by Speedo, while fending off Long John's attacks. I enquired about the Macaws and the aviary. When Menagerie lady smiled sweetly and fluttered her lengthy eye lashes. I knew I'd been well and truly had.

"It's so very kind of you to house these little friends of mine, but do you mind if I hang on to the aviary? I just can't bear to part with my lovely macaws."

Another lady rang the zoo about rehoming ducks.

"I know you have a large duck pond. I have some pure white Aylesbury ducks, would you like them for your pond? "

Domestic varieties of ducks like Aylesbury's, are almost all descended from wild Mallard. Mallard have one undesirable feature. They are sex mad. They will mate with any other duck. Large, small, living, dead, plastic or rubber. This amorous behaviour, can be witnessed every spring around parks, rivers, lakes and canals.

Therefore it's inadvisable to mix domestic ducks with wild species, as they interbreed and produce hybrids. The zoo's ducks consisted of pure bred wild species, such as Mandarins, Carolinas and Teal. These are usually termed ornamental ducks. A term used to distinguish between, the ducks you put on a lake or pond and the ones that you place in an oven dish.

I attempted to explain, "I'm afraid I'm unable to house your ducks in our collection, as all our ducks are ornamentals."

"Well I never" she said, "I've only seen them through the fence when I walk my dog, but I could have sworn they were real."

It never ceases to amaze me how little the general public know about their native wildlife.

A lady from north Wales, rang the zoo concerning a hand raised male blackbird called Blackie. Apparently, he had always been silly tame. But he had now turned aggressive towards her husband Delwyn, attacking his bald head at every opportunity.

This was very unusual behaviour. However, when birds become imprinted on humans, they can exhibit extremely possessive behaviour. It sounded as if Blackie having reached sexual maturity, now saw Delwyn's wife as his mate and Delwyn, or at least his head as an adversary.

The attacks had now become so violent, Delwyn wore his motor cycle helmet indoors at all times.

Wilf, an elderly member of our bird staff, who had a tame song thrush and other avian waifs and strays, agreed to home Blackie.

Blackie's guardians agreed. A few days later a unusually large cardboard box, virtually covered in heavy duty gaffer tape, arrived at the zoo. When it was finally opened, out hopped not a blackbird, but a full grown Raven. Which explained why Delwyn wore a motor cycle helmet. This now posed a problem for Wilf, Blackie's new owner. Despite apparently having a lush head of hair, Wilf also had sideburns which suspiciously curled outwards.

And out of earshot the younger keepers referred to Wilf, as Wiggy Wilfred. Would Blackie detect under Wilf's inanimate head covering, there lurked yet another adversary ?

Despite a number of native birds being colourful, with some like the green woodpecker, jay and bullfinch even rivalling tropical birds. It's often assumed any colourful wild bird at liberty is a zoo escapee.

"It must be one of yours," is the phrase often used.

"There's one of your tropical birds in my garden."

"What does it look like?"

"Definitely tropical. It's a reddish colour, walks about quickly and looks intelligent. It's the sort of bird you would expect to see in one of those African wildlife programmes, walking on the back of a hippopotamus."

"Any idea of the size?"

"Let's see, about the size of two large cows, with a much bigger head."

"Not the hippo the bird."

"Smaller than a duck. But bigger than a sparrow. I know that's a bit vague. But it's definitely not a wild bird, it's too tame. It must be one of yours."

The caller's house was close to the zoo and I arranged to visit on my way home. When I arrived. I was grilled at the front door.

"If you're from the zoo, how come you don't have any identification?"

"We only spoke ten minutes ago."

"I'll let you in this time, but next time I'll need to see your ID."

Reluctantly, I was lead into the back garden, where an audience of gnomes were waiting.

"There's the bird, on the lawn near Eric."

"Eric? "

"The one armed gnome with the wheel barrow."

"That's a chaffinch."

"How did it get out? It's a very quick walker, I supposed it sneaked out?" The red mist descended.

"It didn't sneak out, or escape by any other means, it's one of the commonest British birds. Are there any other wild birds in your garden, you think may have escaped from our zoo? Oh look there's a blackbird, he's walking about looking intelligent, must be one of ours."

"Alright! there's no need to be sarcastic, How was I to know it wasn't an escaped bird ? I'm not an orthodontist"

"Koi carp are not cheap!" The caller bellowed down the phone.

"I immediately thought this was a sales call and thanking the caller for the information, was about to hang up."

"Your stork, identical to the one on the margarine container, has been flying into my garden every night and eating all my yamato-nishikikis. The pond is now devoid of fish, they are all inside your stork."

"But we don't have any storks in the zoo."

"Of a night time, our pond is illuminated by lights and they are automated to change colour. Madge and I like to sit and watch the fish and guess which coloured light is going to appear next. This magic moment is shattered, when your stork appears and descends into our garden scaring the heck out of Madge. The pond lights produce giant shadows and your stork with its wings outstretched looks just like a Terry-duck-tile."

"If I could just emphasise? We don't have any storks at the zoo, not one, never have."

It was no good, it was like talking to the TV.

"The stork glares at us, then licking his beak, wades into the pond and starts stabbing at the fish. He never misses, you would think he had a harpoon."

Speaking in train station announcer mode, I tried to get my message across.

"Attention! There are nineteen species of stork in the world. In our zoo, the grand total is nil! We are utterly stork-less."

"He gulps em down whole without chewing, pure greed.

Nothing but pure greed. One night we scared him after he had swallowed some of the fish, then he opened his beak and regurgitated yamato-nishikikis all over the decking before flying off. I had to give them CPR and the kiss of life, before putting them back in the pond. They made a full recovery. Then the next night, he came back and ate the lot."

At this point I had just got into the rhythm of chanting. "We don't – have no storks, we don't – have no storks. What have we got? We ain't got storks." Suddenly the caller had tuned into my wave length.

"Are you saying you don't have any storks?"

"I did happen to mention that in passing, yes."

"Well what's them grey things on stilts, near the entrance to the zoo?"

"Demoiselle Cranes."

"That's the ones I'm talking about! The Mademoiselle Crakes, one of them, probably the fattest one, has had all my yamato-nishikikis away. I raised them from small fry and I'm totting up the cost now. I want compensation. I'm a fair man. I'm not going to claim for pain and suffering. But I could mind. If I as much as mention fish Madge fills up."

Not being sure of my life expectancy, I had to bring closure to this conversation.

"Can we just clarify something? The demoiselle cranes are pinioned. They can't fly. They are grounded, feet permanently on terra firma. Unable to rise in the air and leave the enclosure, unless assisted by a tornado."

The problem with this conversation, the caller was repeating what I said to his wife. Then relaying her questions back to me.

"He said they are opinionated Madge, they can't fly. It's to stop 'em getting caught up in tornados. I'll ask him. Madge says our house backs onto the zoo and there is a public footpath at the end of our garden. Madge says with their long legs, those crakes could have jogged over here, done a spot of fishing and got back before you missed them?

"No they couldn't! The cranes can't get out of the enclosure, it's ringed by a seven-foot fence. And before Madge asks, they can't jump or burrow, nor are they let out for the weekend. The bird that almost certainly ate your fish is a heron. A wild fish eating British bird, that frequents rivers, streams and other waterways. And tell Madge we have as many herons at the zoo as we do storks.

"So it's a sort of swan then."

"No it's nothing like a swan."

"A fish eating swan Madge."

"Forget swan! A heron is a long legged grey bird with a dagger like beak."

"More of a pelican type bird then. It's a pelican Madge. Those birds you describe as having a bag for life under their chin."

"No, it's a heron type bird. That's why it's called a heron.

Herons will hunt at night and are attracted to fish ponds where there are lights"

"I wish you'd told me this before. You've been wasting our time." (why are people surprised there are teeth marks on my desk?)

"And you're positive the culprit is a heron type wild bird, flying around of a night time stealing fish from fish ponds."

"Positive."

"Well I never, I thought only owls flew at night. He said it's definitely not a swan or a pelican Madge. It's a heron Madge. They frequent rivers and streams. I'll ask him. Madge asks would the water company pay compensation?"

THE KOOKABURRA AND
THE BICYCLE REPAIR KIT

The bird garden was adjacent to a golf course. When the peacocks went walkabout, they trooped off in single file, taking a scenic route.

The procession ending up on the golf greens where they sun bathed for the rest of the day. This regularly got me in to hot water with Mr Pettigrew the golf club secretary. An officious short rotund man. Who resembled the plastic men minus the smile, you'd expect to find at the bottom of a budgie cage. (An ideal location for him.)

I'd had one run in with him already, about the peafowl loitering on the golf greens.

I'd called him a pompous miniature jobs worth and for some reason he'd taken offence.

"Mr Naylor there was an emergency committee meeting regarding livestock who trespass on golf greens."

Stifling my yawns, I feigned interest.

"And what was the conclusion of the meeting Mr Pettigrew?"

"A unanimous decision, none of our members are going to stand for it. You know what that means?"

"You're all going to sit down."

"It means a fine will be issued every time the peacocks trespass."

"I'll inform the peacocks."

We hoped the peacocks would remain in the bird garden following the arrival of four attractive peahens. These were confined for two months in a covered enclosure, to inhibit their wanderlust. Without taking this precaution they would head for the horizon and keep going. This was frustrating for the peacocks who paced up and down outside the enclosure, displaying their feathers, making amorous eye contact and counting the days.

I hoped I'd heard the last from Mr Pettigrew. But then the kookaburra escaped.

"We have bird trouble on the golf greens again Mr Naylor.

After my complaint about the Peacocks you have obviously taken your revenge."

"Revenge, in what way Mr Pettigrew?"

"Don't pretend you don't know anything about a giant woodpecker who has obviously been trained to steal golf balls. How can golfers concentrate on their game when balls are being interfered with?"

It was time to eat some humble pie, well at least take a nibble.

"I'll come over and catch the kookaburra"

"What about the woodpecker?"

"I'll catch him too."

The kookaburra had escaped, when Nick a bird keeper who was always more interested in conversation than the task at hand, left the aviary door open. The next day while demonstrating to another keeper how the kookaburra had escaped, the remaining kookaburra did likewise. Nick was philosophical.

"At least they are both together now."

The phone rang shortly afterwards.

"You said you were coming over. We now have two giant woodpeckers stealing golf balls."

"I'm on my way Mr Pettigrew."

"You better had be. I don't want them breeding into a flock."

The kookaburras were in their element on the golf course. The long grass adjacent to the tees contained voles, field mice and slow worms. Kookaburras will not only eat anything that moves, but also inanimate food. The largest of the Kingfisher family, known as the 'Laughing Jackass, ' due to its cackling laugh, can be heard on the soundtrack of many exotic films, regardless of the film's location.

No longer a bird of the Australian outback. Kookaburras are

now found in the suburbs of Australian cities and are not averse to stealing sausages and chicken legs from barbeques.

In the absence of barbeque food, we tried to trap the birds using a cage filled with white mice. But the kookaburras weren't interested in rodents, even albino ones.

Nick had an idea, a frequent occurrence. But a useful idea from Nick usually coincided with the appearance of Hailey's comet. Nick explained, as best he could, with his usual speech impediment, a mouth full of small square peppermints.

"Kookaburras love snakes, so we inflate the spare inner tube I have in this bicycle repair kit. Paint a zigzag pattern on it and drag it through the grass. We then catch the kookaburras when they swoop down for the kill."

In theory it could work. Kookaburras will attack python road kills on Australian highways. But they can become so preoccupied in beating and stabbing the lifeless reptile, they sometimes end up becoming road casualties themselves. After cutting and tying the inner tube at each end, inflating it and decorating it with a zigzag pattern we dragged the snake-like decoy through the grass.

From above we were watched by the kookaburras who were already bobbing their heads with excitement. The male dived and landed alongside the inflated prey, after repeatedly stabbing at it, our snake hissed loudly and deflated. Nick quickly grabbed the bird and plunged him into a bag before securing it. The female kookaburra swooped. But it was more interested in revenge than hunting. Landing on Nick's shoulder it hammer drilled the side of his head with its beak. Nick spurting peppermints fainted. The kookaburra continued the attack, treating Nick like just another road kill until I restrained it and placed it in a second bag. At that moment a golfer appeared.

"So you've caught the woodpeckers. Oh dear what's up with your colleague?"

"He got pecked, then fainted." Gazing at Nick laying next to his scattered peppermints the golfer shook his head.

"I never knew woodpeckers were that vicious, it's knocked all his teeth out."

IN PURSUIT OF THE SNAKEBIRD

Having a strong Cumbrian accent, with a tendency to mumble and digress on to unrelated subjects most of my conversations are one sided and take place with puzzled, furrowed browed individuals who usually escape, by waving to an invisible friend, before making a getaway. What has this got to do with the snakebird you may ask? The snakebird and my poor communication skills, were the cause of a misunderstanding that occurred, when I was studying birds in outback Australia, for the British Museum of Natural History.

Australia has less bird species than many similar sized continents, but as with its plants and animals, its bird life has great diversity and uniqueness. Sixty per cent of the 250 odd Australian birds, occur nowhere else. It's truly a bird lover's paradise, where you can see and hear multi-coloured parrots, kookaburras that cackle like hyenas and lyrebirds who impersonate everything, from chain saws to car alarms.

This particular day, the other members of the expedition team had gone into town for supplies. I was banned from these excursions for good reason. My accent, was impenetrable to Australians. Invariably when I requested an item in a shop, even though I emphasised every word precisely, with the facial contortions of a Maori war dancer, the assistant would after much scratching of the head, retreat to a back room and wait for me to leave. Consequently it was norm for me to be left at camp or in the field. While my colleagues bought supplies and investigated the delights on offer, in outback towns with one shop, a pub and a post office. (Where usually the same guy took turns sitting behind the counters of all three establishments).

One of the expedition's tasks was to find an anhinga, whose other name is darter, but you might be interested to know is also called the snakebird.

These large prehistoric looking fish-eating birds, frequent rivers, lakes and other areas of water. Anhingas swim with their body below the surface and their heads held serpent-like out of the water. They could have been christened the drowning stork bird, but snakebird got the vote.

So here I was, scanning the area with my binoculars for a snakebird. Knee deep in the water of a large billabong, (Aussie for pond.) Fending off horse flies, mosquitoes and pulling leeches from parts of my body that other parasites couldn't reach. Every time I struggled to haul myself out of the water, the leeches fought to pull me back. In the heat the slightest exertion caused fatigue and I regularly slumped down on a fallen log to get my breath back. The ever-present danger in outback billabongs, is that a 'saltie', a salt-water crocodile, the largest reptile in the world, which can exceed twenty feet, will be sharing the water with you.

Out of the water crocodiles can move at human jogging speed and will travel over land from one area of water to another. Given that, I suppose you're just as much at risk from a crocodile attack waiting at a bus stop, or buying a paper, as you are wading in a billabong. But knee deep in murky waters, you feel more vulnerable. Every ripple takes on a sinister shape and you're always aware, just one bite from those massive jaws could render you three feet shorter.

Once the image of a crocodile has taken root in your mind, you start to imagine every object is a camouflaged crocodile, including the log you're sitting on. Hence the habit I had of regularly looking between my legs.

I heard humming gradually getting louder, fearing a mosquito was stuck in my ear; I kept slapping the side of my face, until a moving cloud of dust indicated a vehicle was approaching. In the Australian desert heat, mirages are common, the landscape shimmers and comes alive, pools of water appear on roads, in trees. You're likely to see kangaroos on skateboards, Koala Bears on pogo sticks. Well let's just say your brain plays tricks with your eyes.

Consequently I was well prepared to ignore this vehicle, even if it turned out to be an ice cream van playing a familiar theme tune. Suddenly a battered and beaten four by four, raced out of a dust cloud and screeched to a halt. An ultra large Aussie, his physique bursting out of his shirt and shorts, leaped out of the truck without opening the door. Just the sort of stunt I detest. Simply because if I attempted it, I would qualify for a ride in an ambulance.

This guy was bronzed, polished and buffed. It must definitely be in the Aussie genes. I had three skin colours, boiled eggshell, blue and red, with blotched variations of all three. Even in the stifling heat of Australia I never wore shorts. There was a reason. On my first day in Oz I did don a pair of Bermudas. Slapped half a pound of zinc cream on my nose and felt part of the surfing community. Until, a tactful Aussie nudged me in the ribs and loudly enquired,

"Which dead bloke did you borrow the legs off ?"

My bronzed Aussie visitor towered over me, blocking out the sun like an eclipse.

"What you afta mate?" I was about to say anhinga, but I thought the colloquial name snakebird would make me more easily understood. I spoke as slowly and as precisely as I could. I had an advantage, we were alone in the outback and he couldn't pretend to spot a friend, wave and escape.

"I'm looking for a snakebird. A snakebird."

I emphasized. "That's a snakebird. Snake ..Bird."

He slapped me on the shoulder, almost shoving me back in the billabong.

"You seem pretty desperate. I know just the place, jump in."

Amazing! He understood me first time. What a stroke of luck to have met a guy who knew where to find snakebirds, who is also fluent in mumble. My pronunciation must be getting better, or we were related.

I bounced around in the speeding truck, trying to maintain a pleasant smile, even though I was regularly hitting the cab roof and facing in a different direction every time I landed. All I could see was red dust. Although the windscreen wipers were working overtime, they had little effect as there was no windscreen. Eventually we drew up outside a lonely run down café, with a towering sign bigger than the building, "Eat Ere Or Starve."

A smile cracked open my dried thick red make-up.

"Are we here?"

My colleague nodded towards the building.

"There you go mate."

"What about the snake bird?"

"You're looking right at her. Best flaming snack bar for miles."

WATERCRESS SAM

Zoological Gardens like any other working environment have their share of eccentric and anti-social individuals. Some are attracted to working with non humans, due to disillusionment with their own species. One such person was a penguin keeper called Leslie, who insisted on being called Clint. A homage to the movie icon, who he believed he resembled. Even though, Leslie was two foot shorter and four stone heavier than Mr Eastwood. If anybody addressed him as Leslie, it usually ended in a stand off. Late in Leslie's career, name badges were issued to all keepers, but he would brusquely tell any zoo visitor who addressed him as Leslie, "Don't wind me up, the name's Clint. Always has been, always will be."

Leslie, sorry Clint refused to communicate with the public.

If someone asked when the penguins were due to be fed, he would march the questioner over to the sign displaying this information. Stab each stencilled word with his finger, before pressing his cheek against the sign and smiling maniacally.

With some keepers it wasn't so much dislike of the public more irritation.

Jamie, a bird of prey keeper, once caused a PR firestorm when he was feeding the vultures and being teased unmercifully by a group of school children. An occupational hazard all zoo keepers have to endure, when working inside an animal cage or enclosure. The children were repeatedly asking Jamie what type of vulture he was. This was a sore point with Jamie. Being bald except for wispy strands of hair and having a large red hooked nose, hunched shoulders and size ten feet. Jamie was ultra conscious his silhouette resembled that of a feathered carrion eater.

One of the schoolchildren seemed sympathetic
"I don't think you look like a vulture at all."
At last a sympathetic voice he thought. Then she let fire.
"I think you're more like a Marabou Stork."
The Marabou Stork, with its large bald head, long beak and pendulous skin hanging from its throat, has to be the ugliest stork. Uglier than many vultures.

Jamie was incensed and determined to get his own back. He informed the children that zoo keepers love their job so much, when they die, they donate their bodies to the zoo freezer. Taking a large piece of bloody rib cage from the vulture food bucket, he passed it by the faces of the open mouthed children. Before throwing it to the vultures, who enthusiastically tore it apart. Jamie grinned.

"That children, was old Horace, one of our bird of prey keepers. Old Horace always enjoyed the vultures. Now as you can see, the vultures are really enjoying old Horace."

Needless to say there was a storm of protests. The zoo hastily issued apologies to the school and parents of the traumatised children. Jamie was suspended pending an enquiry. Old Horace the bird of prey keeper, was a well-known malingerer and seized this opportunity to seriously malinger. He demanded expert counselling for being rumoured deceased and his remains laid to rest in the vulture food bucket. He went off on sick leave, from which he never returned.

Talks, guided tours and demonstrations are now an important part of every zoo visit. Zoo keepers equipped with microphones, give polished performances often in purpose-built arenas. When I was a young keeper, an informal unrehearsed tour by a zoo keeper, was all that was available to visitors. The tour terminated when the tour guide ran dry of information, or the visitors on the tour lost interest and disbanded. You knew your tour was not going well, when there was only one person in your party and they were doing a newspaper crossword. This happened to me one wet January. After traipsing past empty cages and enclosures, where the inmates had the good sense to keep out of the weather. I asked the guy if he wanted to continue. "No by all means keep doing what you're doing, my train doesn't go to till three."

Giving talks to visitors can be full of pitfalls, even for the experienced zoo man. Thomas Gillespie, the founder director of Edinburgh Zoo, famous for its penguin collection, was giving a guided tour to a group of zoo directors. He was eager to demonstrate that King Penguins will never pick up a dead fish. They would rather starve than do this and have to be force fed in captivity. Thomas emphasised this in his dramatic introduction, before throwing a herring at the feet of a king penguin. The penguin promptly picked up the fish and swallowed it. The only time this has been witnessed before or since.

A guided tour round the zoo by one zoo keeper was simply an opportunity for him to talk about his budgerigars. Illustrated by photos he would hand round. When anyone asked questions about the animals in the cages and enclosures, they were being led passed Max would always bring the conversation back to budgies.

"An elephant is just big and grey, that's all there is to it. But budgies, they come in so many colours, as you can see in this next batch of photos."

When giving tours you always had to think quickly on your feet and be ready with an answer, no matter how stupid the question.

"Where would I find the extinct birds?"

"They will be in the empty aviaries, you can't miss 'em."

Lenny was an introverted keeper and his tours around the bird section were an ordeal for everyone concerned. He became tongue tied when asked questions and resorted to simply reading aloud the scant information from the signs on the cages.

"I wish I could make the tour more interesting Bill."

I advised Lenny to tell an anecdote and told him the story of the ancient Greek playwright Aeschylus who died when a lammergeyer dropped a tortoise on his head. Lammergeyers, a type of vulture, air lift bones, dropping them on rocks from a height, to enable them to feed on the exposed marrow. They also occasionally do this with small animals including tortoises. Aeschylus had a premonition that his house in the mountains would burn down on a certain day and he would die. On the day in question, he spent all day sitting outside his house. A Lammergeyer air lifting a tortoise, mistook Aeschylus's bald head for a rock and tortoised him. Lenny loved the anecdote.

"Great I'll tell that story, at the Lammergeyer aviary. But I'll never remember the Greek guy's name."

"Just say the first Greek name that comes into your head, no one will know."

On the next tour, Lenny was unusually confident, ending his tour at the Lammergeyer aviary, where he told the tortoise anecdote.

"And that people is how the ancestor of the lammergeyer you see here, caused the death of that famous Greek philosopher, Demis Rousoss"

(Forever and ever)

The most antisocial zoo keeper I came in contact with, was Watercress Sam, a hippo keeper. Hippos weigh up to three tons and voraciously eat and rapidly digest tons of fresh vegetation. The end result is as bad as you can imagine. Made worse by the Hippos habit of scattering their faeces everywhere, with a rapid motion of their loo brush-shaped tail.

Even though the water in their enclosure is cleaned frequently, it's invariably polluted. For this reason, some zoos refuse to keep hippos. Sam loved hippos. And most of Sam's personal habits were as unsavoury as the animal he worshipped. The original colour of his zoo uniform was undetectable and his body odour surrounded him like an aura. On hot summer days even the baboons would hold their noses when Sam walked by. While skunks would nod their heads, respectfully, acknowledging Sam could produce a more potent scent than they could. Sam's trademark was his waist high waders. These he wore winter and summer. On one rare occasion when he had taken these off, a thriving aquatic plant was observed entwined around his sock. Apparently growing in a medium that didn't bear thinking about. Legends spring from such incidents and from then on he became known as 'Watercress Sam.'

Sam's interest in animals was pretty limited. He liked hippos, more hippos and little else. The walls of Sam's room in the Hippo House were covered with hippo photos. From brown faded black and white prints, to more recent ones in colour. There were studies of hippos indulging in every type of hippo activity, not all of them pleasant.

When a new enclosure was being built. Sam's predictable comment would be, "Hippos would look good in that." Sam's dream, was the zoo would be developed into a hippo park, from which the public were excluded. Sam was not a people person.

When visitors came through the turnstiles he would growl.

"How many more of them are there? They just pile in here as soon as the sun shines, then just hang about the place."

If a visitor approached Sam with an enquiry, he always attempted a quick getaway.

An assertive American tourist once cornered him waving her zoo guide in his face.

"Now keeper! Where might I find the lions?" Sam looked her up and down and snarled;

"Try Africa!" before striding off, leaving her scanning her guidebook for an exhibit named after the dark continent.

Sam's Yorkshire bluntness, halted most visitor's enquiries in mid sentence, his stock phrase was "I only feed and clean 'em. I don't get paid to talk about habits. Buy a book if thy wants to know about habits." Sam's steadfast refusal to dispense information to the public, was the bane of the zoo director. He had the idea of providing Sam with a cassette on the natural history of the hippopotamus, hoping this might encourage him to answer zoo visitor's questions. Sam took to it like a hippo takes to mud and played the tape continuously. Whenever one ventured near the hippo enclosure, the eloquent tones of David Attenborough could be heard at high volume.

"The hippopotamus, also known as the river horse, is semi-aquatic. It can stay under water for as long as twenty-five minutes, aided by specially designed flaps that cover the nostrils.

Herds of hippo will swim as far as twenty miles a day, but mainly feed at night, when they go ashore to graze. Hippos secrete a pink soapy oil that acts like sun block. Protecting their skin from the harmful rays of the tropical sun. Male hippos often have numerous scars, as they regularly fight to defend territories."

Sam had memorised it word for word. Due to constant play, the cassette tape stretched and Sir David sounded slightly inebriated. Some people keep their knowledge to themselves, but Sam became an unselfish dispenser of hippo facts. Whenever a member of the public asked Sam a hippo question, he would unhesitatingly provide a wealth of information. Unfortunately the information was never in relation to the question.

"Could you tell me how old are the hippos? "

"The hippopotamus, also known as the 'river horse,' can stay under water for as long as twenty five minutes."

"What do you feed the hippos on?"

"Herds of hippo will swim as far as twenty miles a day, but mainly feed at night when they go ashore to graze."

"That's not what I asked."

"If you think that's wrong, see David Attenborough. I'm only the lecturer"

Around this time, a charming, handsome and knowledgeable youth, joined the staff of the zoo. I thought I had landed a plum job, when I became zoo supervisor. But the office and transport, turned out to be a table in a storeroom and use of an ancient bike.

I was less of a supervisor and more a general dog's body. The go-between the director and keepers. Every morning, I would cycle around the zoo. Visiting the Bird House, Monkey House and other zoo sections. Relaying the head keeper's requests and moans, (mostly moans,) back to the director. The head keepers were much older than I and a few resented me.

I was eager to impress. Sam being the only member of staff on the hippos, he was automatically a head keeper, so I had to win him over too, but it was an uphill task. Every morning I cycled past the Hippo House and waved to a stony faced Sam. If I slowed down prepared to talk, he usually turned his back.

Having worked in an African national park, I decided to impress Sam with my hippo experiences and hopefully bond. Aware of Sam's lack of personal hygiene, the bonding would be undertaken from a hygienic distance.

As I approached the Hippo House on bonding morning, the voice of David Attenborough could be heard loud and clear in the still morning air. Sam was in his favourite position, waist deep in the polluted water of the hippo pond, demolishing a large sandwich, while leaning on his long handled broom.

He'd watched me cycle up the hill and as I got nearer he thrust the sandwich in his overall pocket. Bowing his head, he began to stir the water with his broom. Aware he would find it hard to avoid me, I dismounted and leaned my bike up against the hippo fence. While Sam continued muttering in unison with Sir David.

"Good Morning! It's Sam isn't it?"

"Aye."

"Handsome pair of hippos you have there Sam."

Sam still kept his head down. Muttering "I know."

"I'm Bill the new supervisor. I expect you've heard. What do you like most about Hippos Sam?"

Sam mumbled. "Hippos secrete a pink soapy oil that acts like sun block, protecting their skin from the harmful rays of the tropical sun."

"Fascinating animals, but quite dangerous hey Sam? More people killed every year by hippos than by lions. I've studied them in the wild you see."

Sam, obviously agitated, began to swirl his broom quickly around in the water.

"No thy hasn't."

"I have, yes Sam."

"No way!" He shouted, shaking his head.

I was becoming quite irritated. "I can assure you I've studied them in the wild." Sam threw his brush aside, waded across the pool, climbed out of the water and faced me through the chain link fence. He was so close, the pervading aroma brought tears to my eyes, even obscuring the smell of the hippo pond.

"See now young fella. You've never studied them in the wild. And I'll tell you why I know. I've been here twenty five years and those hippos have never escaped once."

SNAKES ALIVE

Since the book of Genesis, when a serpent wrecked a young couple's garden party, snakes like politicians, have long been associated with evil and treachery. Describing someone as a snake in the grass, automatically labels him or her as a sneaky individual.

The character assassination of serpents continued through the centuries. Hollywood must share some blame. Churning out a succession of western films, where Red Indians with dodgy accents and fake suntans, accuse every low standing character of speaking with a forked tongue. But the notoriety snakes have acquired is totally undeserved. The majority are inoffensive and would rather avoid human contact. Out of the almost 3000 species of snakes, only around one in a thousand are venomous. The popular misconception, is snakes never miss an opportunity to get their fangs into somebody. However most fatalities from snake bites, occur in countries where it's customary to go without shoes. There are gung-ho types, who also succumb to snake bites, when attempting to catch a snake to impress.

The speed at which a snake can strike is so swift, the only movement the human eye witnesses, is the recoil following the snake's strike. The very reason many self styled snake hunters think the snake hasn't connected. They are the ones who punch the air and shout "missed!" before collapsing in a heap.

Snakes alongside spiders, are the most common animal phobias.

A person in the grip of snake phobia can act in the most outlandish fashion. A lady once rang the zoo, demanding a meeting with the person in charge of the reptiles.

Being that person, I invited her to meet up in the Reptile House.

She was aghast at this suggestion.

"I'm not setting one foot inside a snake depository." Instead we arranged to meet on the nearby lawn. Where the lady enveloped in a large fur coat, sporting a wide brimmed hat, eventually appeared.

"You are no doubt aware I am Lady Mulberry-Smythe. Having just moved into 'Roselands,' I'm concerned that I'm now within close slithering distance of your cobras and boa conductors. What assurance can you give, that if one escaped it would be quickly apprehended?"

I tried to lighten the mood.

"It would be caught in no time. We would simply follow the trail of bodies."

Having missed her funny bone by a mile. The fur lady swung her fox fur stole tightly around her neck. "I can't understand why these slimy obnoxious things are kept in a zoo. They are of no obvious use to anybody. They just spend their lives poisoning and squeezing anybody who comes within reach of their squeezers and fangs, they're simply evil!"

"Lady Mullberry, if a snake escaped it's unlikely you would be in any danger. Most people's fear of snakes is based on misunderstanding. Snakes are largely un-aggressive and certainly not slimy, have you ever held one?" The fur lady stepped back and shuddered.

"I wouldn't soil my hands on such creatures. Obviously nothing has been achieved by our meeting. I will have to write to the zoo trustees and demand to know why they are providing cages for these dangerous slimy creatures, when there are cats who need homes."

Considering her chronic dislike of all things cold blooded, Lady Mullberry had not chosen the ideal location for our meeting. A snake handling session was in progress at the far end of the lawn, near the zoo exit. Snake enthusiasts were taking it in turn to handle a small python. Pythons though muscular, when handled regularly, usually become tame, rarely bite and are ideal for introducing even small children to snakes.

Lady Mulberry bid me good day, turned on her heels and

obliviously strode towards the exit where the snake-handling group was assembled.

"Coming through, make way." She demanded. A girl with a python draped around her shoulders, assumed Lady Mullberry wanted a turn in handling the snake and obligingly placed it around her shoulders.

Perhaps thinking she had been presented with a garland of flowers. Lady Mullberry held both ends of the snake, smiled at the circle of faces, mouthing the words,

"How kind." It was not until the flickering forked tongue was darting inches from her face did she realise the horror of all horrors had visited itself upon her. She was joined with snake. Her face drained of all colour, as facial muscles began to twitch involuntarily.

I pushed my way through the group to try and retrieve the snake, but was too late. It disappeared within the large fur coat.

In an effort to dislodge the unwanted serpent, I shook Lady Mullberry by the shoulders Her hat, broaches and earrings hit the floor, but the snake remained concealed. She grabbed my shoulders and yelled,

"More shaking, more shaking!" Gripping her lapels, I shook her with all my might. Cross-eyed and dishevelled, she looked as if she'd been hang-gliding at high altitude for a week, but there was no sign of the snake.

I thrust an arm inside the fur coat and rummaged around. I then pushed my head inside and performed advanced rummaging. Lady Mullberry waited till my face emerged and to emphasise no permission had been given for a body search, slapped the emerging face hard. Suddenly she froze, eyes wide, legs apart, clamping her hands on my shoulders.

The python's head had appeared just below the hem of her skirt. Lady Mullberry decided this was time to bring in reinforcements. Wrenching the stole from her neck, she proceeded to attack the snake with the deceased fox. The python descended, entwining itself around her ankle. Lady Mulberry had now forsaken all decorum and went into high kicking routine, minus the Hollywood smile. This persuaded the snake to tighten it's coils all the more. I begged Lady Mulberry to stay calm. "You must relax, the more agitated, the more you move, the more it will squeeze."

One of the snake enthusiasts provided additional information. "They never stop tightening their coils until the last breath of life has been squeezed out of their prey, then they swallow it."

Lady Mulberry stared down at the python wrapped in a tight ball around her ankle. "You mean it's going to devour my leg?"

Some people talk in tongues when they are hysterical.

Lady Mulberry began to recite her entry in "Who's Who."

"I am the secretary of the Rotary Club, founder member of the townswomen's guild, the wife of a government M.P. I refuse to be eaten by a snake in my husband's constituency."

She then keeled over backwards in a faint. Her body relaxed, the python loosened its grip and I retrieved it. The snake handling participants thanked me for the demonstration, impressed with Lady Mulberry's performance.

"You definitely want to keep her in the act."

A little later in the zoo cafe, I was seated across from a still trembling Lady Mulberry.

"I insist what happened today should be treated in the utmost confidence. Do I have your word? "

I nodded in agreement

"It will not be mentioned to anybody, on condition."

"How dare you blackmail me, after I've been boa constricted ?"

"Lady Mulberry you are a very influential lady. The reptile house gets very little publicity. You may not believe this, but some people don't like snakes. Now, if you could submit a letter to the local paper, saying how much you enjoyed your visit to the zoo's reptile house and perhaps mention your participation in the snake handling session."

"Enjoy! are you serious ? I was almost squeezed into the next life."

"Lady Mulberry, if the local press got hold of the story about you dancing hysterically with a snake coiled on your leg, it could make the front page. Now if you sent a letter of appreciation, as I suggested.

I could then deny any stories that might surface about you dancing with a snake. If you were attacked by a snake, you would hardly praise the staff of the Reptile House would you? That wouldn't be credible."

Lady Mulberry stood up. "Very well, as much as I find it distasteful, I will write a letter as you advise."

She swung the battered stole around her neck but the fox had other ideas, its head detached itself, flying over my shoulder and hitting the adjacent wall.

"Pathetic animal" she sneered, before striding from the cafeteria.

True to her word, Lady Mulberry's letter appeared in the local paper and I sent her a letter of thanks.

"Dear Lady Mullberry-Smythe,

I am writing in appreciation of your letter in this week's Gazette, in which you praised the zoo's snake handling demonstration. As a way of saying thank you, I enclose details of how to sponsor a snake."

(Snake charming Gangnam style)

Because snakes can flatten their bodies and skulls, they are extremely adept at escaping. As a snake obsessed schoolboy, my poor attempts at snake cage construction, meant my snakes spent most of their time exploring the neighbourhood.

I found myself some years later at a newly built zoo, once again catching snakes escaping from poorly constructed snake cages.

A six-foot boa constrictor was the latest to go AWOL. Last seen near the garden of a house adjacent to the zoo. Here lived, an eccentric retired army major, too fond of gin. Although the snake was non-venomous, we were obliged to notify people living in the vicinity.

It was mid-morning, but the major with drink in hand and a beaming smile, was as usual, well lubricated when he answered the door.

"Hallo Zoo-ee keepers. Now did I ever tell you I once shot a elephant while riding a tiger, or was it the other way round?"

"Just thought we'd let you know major, a boa constrictor has escaped from the zoo. It's not venomous, but it can give a nasty bite, so don't attempt to catch it. Phone us if you see it."

Having served in India the major lost no time in giving us his advice on snakes.

"Three tips about snakes. Always remember to empty your boots in the morning. Make sure you keep a hungry mongoose in your bed and what was the other one? Oh yes, keep the fires lit to stop elephants trampling the crops. Now what can I do for you zoo boys?"

It was impossible conducting a conversation with the major, who was living in a different era, in another country and because of his intake of gin probably on another planet.

He vigorously waved us goodbye, stood at his front door, his drink spilling down his shirt and trousers.

"Cheery bye zoo keepers. If I spot that rattlesnake. His rattling days will be over, leave it to me."

By the time we got back to the Reptile House, the boa constrictor had been recaptured and returned to its quarters.

Next morning we received a call from the major. "Pleased to report, fugitive serpent despatched at 1900 hours. Devil of a job nailing the blighter, he was wriggling all over the place. Put up a hell of a fight. The corpse is still lying somewhere on the lawn. Would you be so kind as to remove the wretched thing? We don't want its mate coming in search of revenge do we? Cheery bye zoo boys."

We were puzzled as to what snake the major had killed. The boa constrictor had been recovered and no other snakes were missing. The only other possibility, is that it was a native grass snake. These can grow to four or five feet in length, even longer on the continent.

The mystery was solved, when the major's wife phoned to explain. The previous evening as the sun was going down, she had turned the lawn sprinkler on. As it had a habit of doing, part of the sprinkler head came detached and the hose thrashed about on the lawn.

The major sleeping off a gin and tonic session in his hammock, was awoken by animal noises coming from the zoo. Seeing the hose wriggling about in the moonlight, he took command of the situation. In a moment of bravado and jungle flashback. Just as his wife was turning the water off. He attacked the writhing spitting hosepipe, with a pair of hedging shears. Decapitating eighteen inches from one end.

THE SUBMERSIBLE
ZOO KEEPER

Dealing with escaped animals is often compounded by comments from members of the public, who can never get their head around the fact that if an animal or bird has escaped, it will not be where it's supposed to be. A concerned lady once enquired:

"This green parakeet in the rabbit enclosure feeding alongside the guinea pigs and rabbits. He seems at home, but the other parakeets of the same type are in that aviary over there. Is this one meant to be here?"

"Yes madam he is. But for some reason his colleagues have taken it upon themselves to occupy that aviary."

Zookeepers spend most of their days occupied in the routine of feeding and cleaning. So when animals escape, the adrenalin flows, the hunting instinct kicks in and everyone volunteers to assist in recapturing the fugitives

All kind of calamities can occur during a recapture, the most traumatic I experienced was when Wee Davy, a Scottish bird keeper of small stature almost drowned in the flamingo pond. Davy was small, but over fifteen inches in height, the depth of the flamingo pond. So how could it happen? Read on:

The flamingo pond was adjacent to the penguin pond. A Jackass penguin exploring a gap under the dividing fence decided to swap enclosures for an upgrade. Bigger pond and flamingo pellets which made his face and feet pink. (Flamingos in the wild obtain their pink colouration from the tiny fresh water shrimps they consume. In captivity they have a colorant, carophyll red added to their food.

The same colorant that is added to poultry food that produces pink egg yolks.)

The penguin and the flamingos were a bad mix. Every time the flamingos went in the water, the red-faced penguin would dive in and show off his aquatic prowess by swimming at speed under water. This caused the flamingos to panic and scramble out on the land. Flamingos when harassed run like teenage girls wearing high heels for the first time and it's not unknown for them to sustain sprains and even break their legs. It was imperative the penguin was caught up and returned to his own enclosure.

Wee Davy had little experience of catching birds, so after the flamingos were herded into their hut, a nightly routine to prevent predation by foxes, Davy was assigned the job of catching the penguin. But instead of netting the bird on the land, where penguins walk like contestants in a sack race, he made the mistake of letting it take to the water. Davy, wearing a large pair of waders clutching a long handled mesh net entered the pond. Myself and the other keepers watched on. Catching swimming penguins is virtually impossible. They are in their element in water, while humans are like a fish out of it. The submerged penguin shot about like a torpedo.

Davy, scooping like a hyperactive angler, netting green sludge from pond bottom, suddenly disappeared. We expected him to quickly surface, greener than when he had submerged. But he remained underwater. Bubbles surfacing alongside the net which was being frantically waved from side to side.

Recognising the universal SOS signal for a zoo keeper drowning in a flamingo pond, we jumped in and grabbed the submerged wee Scot. Although there were four of us, getting him on land was like trying beach a full-grown seal and we could only hoist his legs and drag him still submerged through the sludge and out of the pond.

Eyeing his green face, it was obvious the kiss of life would be life threatening to the kisser and probably traumatic to the wee macho Scot.

As the penguin joined us in anxiously waiting for Davy to show signs of life. It was noticeable that the level of the water in the pond had decreased considerably.

This explained the mystery of Davy's weight increase. When he had assumed the horizontal submerged position. His waders had filled with water preventing him rising and then a good proportion of the water in the flamingo pond had been soaked up by Davy's oversize Fair Isle sweater which was now hanging down past his knees, giving him the appearance of a bloated llama?

Davy had suddenly regained consciousness, jabbering incoherently punctuated by recognisable expletives. Thus confirming he had not sustained any injuries, as this was how he normally communicated.

With a hosepipe ban on at the time, we instructed Davy to remain horizontal for a few hours, allowing water to drain from his saturated sweater back into the pond. Davy's horizontal bloated shape now resembled a predatory leopard seal, a penguin's natural enemy. The penguin hurriedly waddled away slithering under the fence back into his enclosure. Job done.

PLUCKING PEACOCKS

The national bird of India, the peacock, has been kept since Roman times as an ornamental attraction. Wandering at liberty in large gardens, the grounds of stately homes and palaces. Unfortunately, peacocks have a tendency to go 'walkabout.' And when they wander where they're not supposed to be wandering, that's when problems start.

The peacock is a born show off, as well as displaying its magnificent fan shaped feathers to prospective mates. It also displays to chickens, dogs, lawnmowers, telephone boxes and other objects. Peacocks like all male pheasants will fight other males and if a peacock sees its reflection in a glass door, it will attack the 'opponent' with a flurry of kicks worthy of a kick boxer. Expensive damage has been done to cars, when peacocks have attacked their mirror image in the shiny bodywork.

While bird song is usually musical and pleasant, a peacock's call is reminiscent of a car alarm and it goes off frequently. Peacocks call to communicate with other peacocks. They also call when rain is imminent, thunder is heard, a plane flies overheard, or to greet a passing train. In fact any unusual sound will start them off. If they don't hear an unusual sound, they just call to stay in practice.

Although peacocks are traditionally kept as liberty birds, they are certainly not the gardener's friend as they relish many types of garden plants and flowers.

They also dig in garden beds, then lie in the excavated ditch and kick soil over their feathers. This feather cleansing routine which many birds indulge in, is known as 'dust bathing,' which rids the plumage of parasites. I once had a distraught lady almost in tears. approach me at the zoo.

"I think you should know, some wicked vandal has half buried one of your peacocks in the flower bed."

Where extensive dust bathing has taken place, the area can resemble a World War 1 battlefield. Many a keen gardener after seeing a peacock's garden make over, must have felt like throwing themselves on the compost heap.

Although there are many privately owned peafowl and some living wild and breeding in the UK. When a fugitive peacock appears as a new bird on the block, it's assumed to be an escapee from the nearest zoo, then the zoo phone never stops ringing.

Zoo birds and animals are now regularly identified with rings, tattoos, microchips and even DNA fingerprinting. But that was not always the case and it was hard to prove a fugitive peacock was not yours. I've been there many times.

The police, besieged by calls, when an escaped peacock is on their patch, just want it caught and don't care by whom. Denying it's your bird, sounds unconvincing, when they produce the evidence

"Peacocks are an exotic bird. An escaped peacock is on the loose. You keep peacocks and other exotic birds, how do you plead? "

"I'll get my net, officer."

A lady rang the zoo to report a peacock in her garden.

"Tara Pennington at 'Shangri-la View' here! One of your Peacockerals has been trying to perch on my bird table. Now it's attacking its reflection in my French windows. When my husband Ralph has apprehended it, would you be so kind as to come and take it away? "

The peacock did not originate from our zoo. But I was obliged to assist, as there were numerous foxes in the area. Peacocks normally roost high in trees. When lost and disorientated however, they will often roost on a low branch, within reach of a fox. And to a fox a peacock is a royal banquet. Catching peacocks is never easy. After hurdling over hedges and scrambling over walls, with spectators advising:

"You will need to get a lot closer if you want to catch it." You feel like a rider-less jockey who is never going to catch his horse.

When you finally have a peacock cornered, they often do a vertical take off. Leaving you red-faced, while the assembled crowd applaud the flying fugitive.

Why not enlist the help of the spectators? you may ask.

The hunting instinct can unleash strange behaviour when civilians become animal trackers. Well adjusted people start blacking up their faces, crawling around in the undergrowth clutching maps, shouting phrases such as "closing in on target at four o'clock."

Some obtain the largest net they can find. Run around frantically looking skywards, until they inevitably run into a tree, or someone else with a large net. I therefore advised Mrs Pennington against attempting to catch the bird.

"If you can lure the peacock inside a garage or shed, by laying a trail of peacock favourites, such as raisins, peanuts, or grapes. I will come and collect it. Please keep me updated on its movements."

This she did, every twenty minutes.

"The peacockeral is now at number 24, Mrs Clarkson's. She tells everybody her daughter is a barrister, but it's common knowledge she's a lap dancer in Leeds. I'll be in touch."

Shortly after, the phone rang again.

"The peacockeral is now at number 30. Where the woman lives who removed the beautiful beech hedge and built the illegal ugly wall. Nobody speaks to her and she wonders why. Over and out."

For an hour there was no news. Then the phone rang.

"The peacockeral is outside our garage, but refuses to go inside.

He's eaten all the grapes and peanuts. We need closure Mr Naylor. Ralph is about to catch it. He's on his hands and knees now, stalking it with a badminton racket and four yards of net curtain."

Peacocks wings are very powerful and need to be held in the folded position to restrain them. I had visions of Ralph apprehending the peacock. And in the ensuing skirmish, ending up swathed in net curtain, hang-gliding over the neighbourhood.

"Please ask your husband not to catch the peacock, he might injure himself."

"Oh Ralph is very capable of restraining wildlife, he was a master butcher."

My ear went numb, as Mrs Pennington yelled the name of a North American Indian down the phone.

"Geronimo! Ralph has caught it. He's caught the peacockeral. He's now putting it in the box our exercise bike came in. Mission accomplished. Your peacock is being packaged and ready to be collected as we speak."

A whole morning had been taken up with the capture of a peacock, that hadn't even escaped from my zoo, while being treated to a detailed social commentary on the Pennington's neighbours.

I arrived at 'Shangri-la View' the Pennington's residence and was escorted by an unusually subdued Mrs Pennington, to the garage where husband Ralph was waiting. Mrs Pennington then swiftly disappeared.

Ralph's clothes and hair were covered in feathers, his face a mass of scratches. Two feathers hanging from his nose twirled as he exhaled. He looked as if he had been tarred and feathered, minus the tar. Alongside him was a large cardboard box from which a peacock's tail was protruding

"So you caught it."

Ralph coughed nervously. "Caught most of it."

I peered inside the box, which contained a mass of blue and green iridescent feathers and a complete peacock's tail. The colourful feathers that make up the famous fan are not actually tail feathers. They are outer tail coverts, feathers surrounding the tail. A peacock's real tail, like the female's, is quite short.

The box contained virtually every feather belonging to a peacock. But the owner of the plumes was absent. As a survival measure, when manhandled, peacocks like other pheasants discard a substantial amount of the feathers. But I'd never seen this amount at the scene of a capture.

Ralph, head downcast, nose feathers twirling, opened the garage door. Out strutted, a very embarrassed oven ready peacock.

HIDING IN PLAIN SIGHT

A number of years ago I was watching a bittern in a Norfolk reed bed. Aware humans were nearby he assumed camouflage mode. Head pointing skywards, he swayed along with the rhythm of the reeds, like a backing singer in a soul band.

Many animals use camouflage, but the Australian Frogmouth deserves an Oscar for its ability to blend into any background. This member of the Nightjar family resembling a wide beaked owl, undergoes a transformation when approached or threatened. Its feet disappear into the plumage; facial plumes cover the beak and its eyes close to mere slits. The body is then contorted, changing shape until it resembles a broken or distorted branch of the tree on which it is perching. When kept in dimly lit aviaries or indoors, frogmouths turn grey, then revert to brown when re-housed in more illuminated accommodation. In Australia young frogmouths that fall from the nest are often 'rescued' and are rehabilitated in zoos. They then have to be hand fed but soon feed for themselves when released. My first day at Adelaide zoo I was instructed to hand feed the frogmouths, all immature rehabs. Their aviary was landscaped with weather beaten tree stumps, to enable them to display their camouflage ability.

Two frogmouths in the aviary had been hand reared from when they were small nestlings. Instead of assuming the shape of a dead log when approached, they greeted every human with a wide open yellow gape and large orange owl-like eyes.

I hand fed them two large mice, placing them in their open mouths and watched them eagerly gulp them down. On returning to the bird room I reported I'd completed the task of feeding the two tame frogmouths. I was then promptly told to return to the aviary and feed the other four frogmouths that were in the aviary.

Although the emu is slower than its African cousin the ostrich, it can still reach 30 mph and side step and use body swerves similar to that of a premiership footballer.

Emus love water and when they encounter a stream will lie on the backs and kick their legs in the air. They are also excellent swimmers, extending their wings on the water surface they dog paddle with their feet.

A little known aquatic habit of emus came to light when I was a trainee zookeeper. A male emu was housed in a mixed species exhibit with a two female zebras. The emu had to be caught up every day to receive an injection and never took kindly to being manhandled by the head keeper and myself.

When grappling with stroppy large birds or animals and attempting to give an injection, it's not unknown for one of more keepers to be injected by mistake, subsequently spending the day comatose or as hyperactive as a hummingbird. After being caught on a daily basis, the emu was wary and would sprint around the enclosure as soon as he saw me.

One particular morning I arrived at the emu enclosure awaiting the arrival of the head keeper. But the emu was nowhere to be seen.

I reacted in the same way you would if your car had been stolen from your garage. I walked out of the enclosure closed the gate, gave adequate time for the emu to reappear, uttered a string of expletives for luck, then went back inside.

Still no emu. I raced back to the bird room. Rehearsing the words that would best explain to my head keeper the emu's absence.

"The emu has completely gone. All of it "

"You've let him out."

"I didn't let him out, I've just sort of misplaced him."

"Misplaced him! He's not a set of car keys. He's a five high flightless bird with size ten feet."

"All I know he's not in the enclosure, at this moment in time "

"Oh really, perhaps he's popped down the shop for a paper. Or an early morning latte."

The head keeper marched me out of the birdhouse.

"Follow me. I'll show you where he is at this moment in time."

In the emu enclosure the head keeper confronted me.

"Still don't know where he is?"

I shook my head.

Staring me sternly in the face, he shot an arm out pointing to the pond.

"Try over there."

Sure enough, the top of a black-feathered head and a pair of eyes were just breaking through the surface of the water like a periscope. The pond was two feet deep but the emu had managed to submerge and remain hidden. It must have assumed this position shortly before I was due at the enclosure. The emu was now the subject of concentrated stares by two keepers and a pair of zebras. Realising his ruse was rumbled. He sheepishly stood up, water pouring from him like a giant sponge, before coming ashore and volunteering for his injection.

JUMBLE JIM AND
THE SHIP OF THE DESERT

Jumble Jim, was one of many self styled, oddball, 'animals experts' that zoos attract.

Claiming to be an ex-big game hunter, with knowledge of animals second only to Noah, he landed a job as a seasonal zoo keeper.

According to Jim, the only animals he hadn't managed to tame or train, he'd wrestled to death. This and other exaggerated claims, were as breathtaking as the inaccurate zoological information that embroidered his endless anecdotes.

"I once financed an expedition to Africa, travelling up the Congo looking for birds of paradise." When it was pointed out birds of paradise are found in New Guinea, Jim never faltered. "Absolutely correct. We proved that beyond shadow of a doubt, we never found one. If you go looking in Africa for birds of paradise, you'll be wasting your time."

Jim acquired the nickname Jumble Jim, from his habit of collecting discarded items from rubbish dumps, bowels of skips and jumble sales.

"You see this old brass ashtray, it once saved by life when I was being chased by cannibals. They had these little spears coated with poison. They were about to take me out for dinner. And I mean take me out. I was the main meal. So I waited in a clearing till they appeared.

When they did, I whips out the old ashtray and dazzles 'em reflecting the sun in their eyes. Within a few minutes they were all seriously dead, job done."

This story seemed far-fetched even by Jim's standards and members of the reluctant audience began to snigger. Jim was most indignant his word was being doubted. "You don't believe me? Think about it. The last thing you want to be doing when you're holding a poisoned spear, is start rubbing your eyes"

Jim irritated the older keepers, who instantly saw through his fictional fabrications and boasts he could tame and train any animal.

"I wouldn't put your face too close to that parrot Jim, he'll have your nose."

"Birds think this big old nose of mine is a beak, what you're witnessing is 'beak bonding.' Give me a week and I'll have this parrot eating out of my hand."

Following his bonding session with the parrot, Jim's nose was bandaged for almost a month. It was quite normal, for him to have parts of his anatomy covered in plasters or bandages. As he was always oblivious to everything, other than the anecdote he was spinning at the time.

Jim was swiftly moved from one section to the other, as it became clear, Jim's story telling was compensation for his inability to complete any work task competently. He lost keys, cleaning tools, left cage doors open and was a total liability. The more he made a hash of jobs, the more exaggerated his story telling became, always ending with the boast. "I had them eating out of my hand in a week."

Jim started work on the giraffe section, the domain of Les Neil, the introverted spectacled head keeper, who was at first amused by Jim's tales.

"I once trained a giraffe to jump fences Les, just like a show jumper. A week was all it took me, I don't think that has ever been done before."

But Les a man of few words, most of them monosyllables, soon tired of hearing of Jim's adventures. Les would chew his pipe audibly and growl, as Jim shared yet another tale of the totally unpredictable with a steady dwindling audience.

Les had no other ambition than to work with giraffes. When you are alongside these unique animals, originally called camel leopards, you realise they are not ungainly or ill proportioned.

Quite the contrary, even though they have enormous strength, (a well aimed kick, or a swing of the head, has been known to kill a lion or hyena), they are graceful and perfectly balanced. Despite being the world's tallest animal, they blend into the background perfectly. Their patterned coat remains unchanged throughout their life, unique to each giraffe, like human fingerprints.

Giraffes, once thought to be almost silent, uttering only the occasional grunt, are now known to communicate like whales, rhinos and other apparently mute species. Using infra sounds, sounds too low for our ears to detect.

The trick question often put to new keepers on the giraffe section, is how many neck vertebrae does a giraffe have? Surprisingly, like us, they possess only seven.

Also on the giraffe section were zebras. Sometimes referred to as horses in pyjamas. But in personality and temperament, zebras are nothing like a horse. A zebra stallion is fearsome and irascible.

Their hooves are so hard, they can't be shod like a horse. When these are overgrown, the zebra has to be anaesthetised and have them trimmed with an electrical sander. In Africa, zebras regularly fend off large predators such as lions and leopards. Consequently they can kick with extreme force, using front or hind feet with deadly accuracy. This was demonstrated to me by Les, who warned me never to put my fingers over the top of a stall occupied by a zebra. Les hung a banana on a string over the stall, where a Grevy's zebra stallion, the largest of the zebra family, had its back to us munching hay.

I hardly saw the zebra move, but after hearing a loud bang on the stall door, the banana was smashed to a pulp.

Camels, Llamas, Alpacas, close relatives of the Giraffe, were also on Les's section. A group of animals noted for their ill temper. Camels, sometimes described as the horse designed by a committee, are brilliantly adapted for life in hot barren country.

These so-called 'ships of the desert' can go up to ten months without drinking. When they do drink, they can consume up to thirty gallons. Camels come in two designs: The dromedary with one hump and the bactrian with two. The humps are often assumed to contain water, but are used to store fat which supply energy when food is scarce. Unlike the dromedary, the bactrian camel grows a thick winter coat, which is discarded in summer. Humphrey, the zoo's male bactrian camel, had a chocolate brown winter coat, that took ages to moult, sometimes all summer. So he was constantly in a state of disrepair, with hair hanging off his back in large shaggy clumps, resembling an old horsehair sofa with its stuffing hanging out.

The look on Humphrey's face, was summed up by Les on being introduced. "That's as happy as he gets."

I never enjoyed being in the same enclosure as a camel. They spit, bite, kick in every direction, lean on you while they urinate down your legs and that's just with people they like. Camels are well aware of the routine when you are trying to clean their quarters, but that doesn't mean they are going to cooperate. Push them backwards and they take a step sideways. It's rather like trying to navigate a giant hairy supermarket trolley, with four wonky wheels.

The preferred means of communication by this Victor Meldrew of the animal kingdom, is moaning. But when a camel opens his mouth you soon forget the complaining, because the first thing that hits you is the awful smell.

A camel's saliva is a concoction of every foul smelling substance you can imagine. A gallon of this vile stuff is kept slushing around inside the camel. And when it wants to demonstrate its displeasure. A generous mouthful of this 'stew' is then ejected at the offending target.

Jim had a few more days left on the giraffe section before he was due to be moved on. Les was counting the hours and trying to find him jobs where he would have to work alone. Sparing the other keepers, the brain numbing effect of Jim's story telling. One job Jim seemed to manage with reasonable competence, was cleaning Humphrey's pen. This had to be swept and the hay and straw replenished twice a day.

On the day that Jim will always remember. Humphrey as usual, had been given a bucket of apples and vegetables to keep him occupied. He munched and moaned, while watching Jim out of the corner of his eye.

Adjacent to Humphrey's enclosure, behind a six-foot wall, was an alcove where Les would write out his daily reports.

Les crept into this area every morning after tea break, hoping Jim would be unaware he was there. Les got away with this for a while, but one morning while Jim was cleaning Humphrey's quarters, he spotted Les tip-toeing into his retreat. From that day Les never had a minute's peace. As soon as he sensed Les was sitting comfortably behind the wall, Jim would begin. "Les! Did I ever tell you about the time I rescued that sheik who was lost in the Sahara ? The one who was dying of thirst. Are you there Les?" Les gritted his teeth. Jim would continue to call out till Les answered.

"Les are you there me old mate?"

Les would throw his pen down, rest his head on the table and reply mournfully "Yes! I'm here. Listening to every word."

"As I was saying Les, this sheik was indebted to me for saving his life, so he gave me twenty camels. Well you know me Les." Les knew what was coming next and mouthed the words.

"It only took me a week and I had em eating out of my hand.

Anyway, I was leaving the country, so I had to sell 'em. What a nightmare Les. Every time I sold one, next morning it would be back outside my tent. I'd trained them so well Les. There was only one thing for it, I had to hypnotise them to forget me. Like I did with that rogue elephant. The one that kept wrecking those villages, the one I told you about Les. The one I learned to ride, the one nobody else could ride Les." Jim's droning monologue continued, picking up strands of other stories that Jim had told many times. Accompanied by Humphrey's moans.

Les for therapeutic reasons, was rhythmically banging his head on his desk, until he suddenly realised there was complete silence!

Jim had shut up and Humphrey had stopped moaning.

Les raced out of the alcove and into the camel house. There was Jim, peddling in mid air, as if riding an invisible bike, his head engulfed in Humphrey's mouth.

Les whipped of his hat and raised it to Humphrey's face,

Humphrey blinked, opened his mouth and Jim covered in green slime, fell to the floor like a bad parachutist.

Les helped Jim to the rest room. While holding his breath to avoid inhaling the obnoxious liquid covering the victim. Jim was unusually speechless, wide eyed and in a daze. There were no injuries, apart from a severely bruised pride. Jim had forgotten the basic rule when you're in an animal enclosure, never take your eyes off the occupant.

Jim left the zoo shortly afterwards. He said he had been hired by the Indian government, to deal with man-eating tigers terrorising villages in the Punjab.

A week later, he was spotted behind a local market stall selling striped furry animals.

Jumble Jim was remembered with fond amusement by all the zoo staff. Whenever his name came up in conversation on the giraffe section, Les would recall with a wry smile.

"Oh yes, Jim was a natural. He was only here a few weeks and he trained Humphrey to pick him up by the head."

AN OSTRICH'S BAD HAIR DAY

Ostriches are always eating, weighing in at 150 kilos and being mainly vegetarian, large amounts of food are required to keep their big boiler of a body stoked up with fuel. Food is always on their mind. Perhaps this is why they swallow a multitude of objects in the mistaken belief it will assist their digestion. Inside a bird that died at London Zoo, was found three foot of rope, a gold necklace and an alarm clock. A bird on a farm in South Africa could have been saving up for a rainy day. Among the items he had swallowed, were 480 assorted coins weighing 8lbs.

The Ostrich, the largest, tallest and fastest running of all birds, requires an athlete's finally tuned physique. Enabling it to cruise effortlessly at 45 miles an hour. But why it chooses to half fill its gizzard with stones, or objects such as spectacles, car keys, pens, gloves and the rest, can only be answered by an ostrich. And they choose to be tight beaked on the subject.

With their notoriety for swallowing objects, I was concerned when the door to the zoo office opened and a large hat worn by a worried looking lady entered.

"So sorry to bother you, but one of your ostriches has swallowed Ginger. I warned him not to stand too close to the animal, I could see what was going to happen and sure enough with a lunge he was consumed."

"Ginger" I enquired.

"Gone" she replied. "So annoying. "

Although parents sometimes yearn for a break from their children, going by her carefree attitude, I assumed she was not talking about a child.

"May I enquire who is Ginger?"

The lady turned to the small nervous man alongside her, wearing a trilby hat.

"Bernard, be so kind as to explain to the zoological keeper would you dear? "

With eyes shooting from side to side, Bernard lifted his hat for a second, revealing a shiny smooth bald head. The lady pointed to this location. "Ginger resided there."

Ginger, it transpired was a hairpiece. A very expensive bright red toupee, identical to Bernard's natural locks, which adorned his head, prior to him becoming too tall for his hair.

"Can the animal be operated on to get ginger back?" Bernard enquired. I tried to soften the blow.

"Well that would not be the usual course of action. Normally the object, in this case Ginger, would be evacuated within twenty four hours. The lady turned to her husband.

"Evacuated, we were evacuated in the war. What is he talking about dear? Do we have to move house to get ginger back?"

"Let me explain, the object will pass through the bird's digestive system in the normal fashion, then be evacuated." The couple gripped each other, with looks of sheer disgust. The man shook his head.

"We couldn't let that happen to Ginger. I mean what kind of animal, eats part of a visitor on a day out to the zoo? Why don't you keep it in a glass tank like the other reptiles?"

"Its not a reptile, it's actually a bird."

"A what? How long have you been in this job? Those pop eyed long necked vandals, run around Africa with all the other man-eaters. And you're keeping and feeding it under the misconception it's a bird. You're an incompetent fool. I aim to sue."

We were now in blame mode and I didn't pin much hope on Ginger's survival, considering what he would have to go through.

As I've mentioned, the gizzard of an ostrich is at anytime half filled with stones and other objects. Following a mangling in the gizzard, he would be exposed to the white water raft ride in highly corrosive digestive juices. After which Ginger would have more

119

than a hair out of place. Forget hairpiece, think hair net. I tried to calm the couple down as best I could.

This was not helped, by the appearance of Mr Atkins, the Bird Curator. Who appeared sporting his trademark beaming smile, which always reminded me of a zebra in mid yawn.

"Hello people, how are we enjoying our visit to the zoo?"

"This is Mr Atkins the Curator of birds. Mr Atkins, the ostrich has swallowed an item belonging to this gentlemen."

"Oh they'll swallow absolutely anything, they are slaves to their gizzards you see." The couple didn't see. The trouble with Mr Atkins, he was a talking book. A large thick volume, that should remain on the top shelf gathering dust.

"That's why they chose ostriches for the Guinness adds, you remember the one with the glass of beverage in the bird's throat. Their gizzards are enormous, like a mass of mill stones. Everything gets churned, mashed, smashed, pummelled and mangled to a pulp."

The curator only stopped talking, when he was lifted off the ground by Ginger's owner.

"My father had red hair, my grandfather and great grandfather had red hair. We can trace our red hair back to William Rufus. If your reptilian vandal destroys Ginger, it will have felled our family tree."

Dancing behind this huddled scrum was a junior keeper, who I at first thought was waving a guinea pig.

"It's Ginger." The lady shouted, as she went into cheer leader mode, clapping hands above her head.

"Ginger's back, Ginger's back!"

Her husband started punching the air spinning on the spot and I too felt the urge to link arms and join the celebration. The junior keeper explained:

"I found it in the adjacent paddock to the ostriches. A visitor said the ostrich was shaking it so violently, it flew out of its beak and landed in the wallaby paddock. One of them was wearing it as a hat."

After being stroked, Ginger was quickly returned to its owner's head, as his wife cupped her hand and whispered in my ear.

"My husband has always had natural wavy red hair. He has never resorted to dye or other artificial aids. I would be grateful if you would remember that, if ever this incident comes up in conversation."

LIGHTS CAMERA MAYHEM

Zoos were once popular film locations. But animals unlike extras don't behave. And a romantic scene is never enhanced by an identity line up of chimpanzee's bottoms. Or a moth-eaten bear scratching areas other bears can't reach, like an enthusiastic banjo player. Star struck keepers also have a habit of 'accidentally' wandering into camera shot and launching into a tuneless song. Demonstrating Britain's zoo keeper's definitely haven't got talent.

Zoo births are always excellent publicity. But nests hidden in dense foliage are not easy to film and I know of one unscrupulous zoo manager who capitalised on this.

In the sixties bird gardens and zoos rarely exhibited birds of paradise, the stunningly beautiful birds from New Guinea who perform dazzling courtship displays. Certainly nobody had bred them. (Including our boss.)

"A TV film crew are coming down to interview you about the breeding success we have had with a bird of paradise."

"But we haven't got any birds of paradise boss."

"You're being negative again. Listen, their nest is in the large weeping fig in the empty conservatory aviary."

"So that's where the birds of paradise we don't have, are nesting"

"Correct. When the TV crew arrive, explain, due to the nervousness of the parents they can't film the nest. Show them this book, tell them the bird of paradise in the photo is the one nesting. Give them some Attenborough style chat, how we are the first to breed them blah blah. But don't let anybody touch the bird of paradise sign on the aviary."

"Why?"

"It's still wet."

"That's deception. You could go to prison"

"You're doing the deceiving. Make it convincing or you could go to prison."

Despite my apprehension the filming went off without a hitch.

The interviewer did a close up of a photo of a bird of paradise in a book. But for most of the news item the camera was trained on an empty bush in an empty aviary.

Next day our boss got a phone call from the manager of a zoo.

"Congratulations on being the first zoo to breed a bird of paradise.

I've a good mind to call the TV company. Remind me again, how many birds of paradise have you got at your zoo?"

Our boss stood his ground.

"I'll let you know that when the eggs hatch."

Escapes were another news item that were sometimes rigged.

Following an escape, a reporter and photographer would arrive expecting to see a fugitive bird. Only to find a keeper in an aviary with a crate, clutching a large net and releasing a bewildered bird which had been bundled into the crate only moments before. The news men were then given an enthralling account of how the 'fugitive' had been chased from county to county before being apprehended. The news team got a front page story unaware it involved a bird that had never left its aviary.

Annual stock taking at the zoo, is often seen on TV. Focusing on a zoo keeper counting locusts. Or standing in a large free flight aviary. Equipped with binoculars and notebook and hastily taking notes. In reality stock taking is chiefly undertaken by checking records. But when 'contrived' is good publicity.

Some years ago, it was decided rather than having a scruffy bird keeper on the news, counting the tropical birds at Chester Zoo's large Tropical House. A bubbly female office worker would be more engaging to TV viewers. Equipped with a notepad and binoculars Tracy from accounts, was dressed in a smart tailored short skirted zoo uniform. Unlike the other keepers, who wore shapeless one size, doesn't fit anybody type uniform.

Tracy was schooled on bird's names, but was more concerned about birds colliding with her bouffant styled hair. Filming took place at a location in the tropical house where nectar bottles attracted hummingbirds up close. The cameras rolled as Tracy with beaming smile gushed about the birds in her midst, but could only remember one bird's name, Robin.

"Which happens to be my boyfriend's name"

"So Tracy why do they call these birds hummingbirds?"

Tracy unaware the whirring of the wings at 80 beats per second earned the hummingbird its name, adlibbed"

"Well, hummingbirds unlike other birds, like robins, can't sing. So they just hum the notes."

"And out of all of the birds you work with, what's your favourite?"

Tracy's head swimming with unfamiliar names like toucan, hornbill and sunbird, fluttered her eyelashes and smiled, before confidently replying:

"For me personally, it has to be the Horny Sunbill every time."

THE PIED PIPER OF
CHISOLM ZOO

In the same way that restaurant owners hate to admit they have cockroaches. "No Mr Health Inspector, I think you will find that they were currants that were rolling around the kitchen floor." Zoo managers dislike having to admit they have rats.

Rats make a beeline for zoo grounds because all the amenities are there.

Food, water and accommodation, plus people who come to look at them. To a zoo keeper, rats are bad news in every way. Not only do they carry a host of diseases. Rats have been estimated to consume a third of the world's stored food. And are successful, because they will eat virtually anything. Living, dead or decaying. They will dive to river beds and feed on mussels, or eat snails to survive harsh winters. They have even been known to chew the nails of elephants. How they trained them to do that I'll never know.

Initially, rats gain access to zoo enclosures attracted by the food on offer. But they will then turn their attention to any animals or birds they can overpower and kill them. When breeding they seek animal protein, become more carnivorous and a greater threat to livestock. These facts were overlooked, by one young zoo superintendent fresh out of university.

This young chap, seemed to be devoid of any practical knowledge of animals. At six foot four, he was the height of ignorance,

Hired simply because he had a degree, as well as a Phd in

sponges. Which led one keeper to comment: "He might come in useful when we scrub down the elephants."

When it became known rats were gaining access to the bird of paradise aviaries and eating their food. The young superintendent decided, until all aviaries could be made rat proof, the bird's food should be removed of an evening. This he reasoned would deter the rats from entering the aviaries. Although he was warned this could pose a risk to the birds, he was adamant his instructions be carried out. The next day six birds of paradise were missing. A search in their aviary, found their partially eaten bodies. Probably one of the most expensive meals rats have ever had.

The hatred that zoo keepers have for rats, has sometimes led to them forming vigilante rat hunting groups. Older zoo keepers recount stories of victorious rat hunts, where many oversize rats were caught. Rat hunters for some reason are given to exaggeration, never describing rats as normal sized. More usually as big as cats. Even larger.

"The rats we caught were so big, we could only carry one per wheelbarrow."

The usual procedure when zoo keepers go rat hunting, is to arm themselves with implements such as shovels and rakes, then search for a rat hole.

Having found an active rat hole, with a well worn path leading to the burrow, the so called 'rat run.' The end of the hosepipe is thrust down the hole and the water turned on. Brown Rats are excellent swimmers, even superior to Water Voles and in experiments have swam for twenty fours non stop.

All eyes are focused on the hole. Complete shush has to be observed. Anybody who as much as sniffs or audibly breathes, is elbowed in the ribs. When the rat burrow has filled up with water, it's a tense moment, as any second the occupant will appear, white water rafting from the entrance.

As soon as there is glimpse of a rat, shovels and rakes come down in a rain of blows. I have witnessed a number of these 'hunts,' and you need a strong stomach to watch the bloody outcome. There are screams of agony, as the weapons collide with heads and limbs and soon the hunters are all horizontal and moaning.

Bruised and bloodied they limp away from the battlefield, cursing their elusive foe. But when wounds have healed, they will hunt another day and no doubt cripple each other again in the repeat performance. Zoo rat hunts, never had much effect on the resident rat population. And despite scientific and technological development of poisons etc to eradicate *Rattus-norvegicus.* The rat population world wide, is unaffected by the all out war declared on it by humans.

One zoo where I was manager, had become a haven for rats, but I was in denial. When anybody ever reported seeing a rat, I would play it down.

"Did this rat look disorientated, or lost? I think you'll find it was a stray"

Within a short time the zoo had more 'strays' than Battersea Dog's Home. So without admitting there was a problem, I decided to trawl for suggestions at the monthly zoo staff meeting.

"There is, I'll admit, a lot of rodents, mostly mice in the zoo grounds. But contrary to rumours, there aren't any, well not many, larger mice type rodents."

"You mean rats?" somebody shouted from the back.

"I'm not going into specifics. And while its not really a problem, if anybody has any ideas on how we could solve this 'ere problem."

"Do you mean rats?" the heckler shouted again.

"I'm open to any suggestions. Thank you."

The head keeper of birds, sitting alongside, was shaking his head.

"Why don't you just get the pest control in? "

"I don't want a conspicuous vehicle driving around the zoo, with rat terminators emblazoned on the side. Visitors will get the impression we have a rat problem. But if you do know of a rat catcher who operates discreetly, put them in touch. "

A week later on returning to my office, I found a tramp in my chair, his feet on the desk, phoning a bet through to the local betting shop.

128

"What the hell do you think you are doing?"

He put a finger to his lips.

"Have a chair I'll be with you in a minute."

"Have a chair! This is my office."

After putting the phone down the intruder swung his legs off the desk.

"Farley's the name, Mr Gaylord I presume."

"It's not Gaylord, it's Naylor."

"Are you sure? Oh well, down to business, what sort of money are you paying ? "

"For what?"

"For ridding your zoo of rats."

"Have you any references?"

"Who from rats?"

"If you don't have any references, how do I know if you are any good?" I regretted asking that question, as a large live ginger rat, in a rusty metal cage, was placed in the middle of my desk,

"Nabbed her, just as she was about to shoot up the drainpipe outside your office door. Female, they are the worse, bite like a terrier. Even a ferret won't tackle a doe rat with young."

The twin aromas of rat and rat catcher permeated the air.

"I wonder if you could put that vermin back from where it came?"

Farley raised his eyebrows. "Up the drain pipe!"

"No, just off my desk."

Farley picked up the cage and put it under his arm, "I'll keep her for study." He said tapping his nose. "Know thy enemy."

"Thank you Mr Farley, I will contact you, if and when I require a rodent exterminator."

"I know what you are thinking Mr Gaylord. You're thinking I look like an undesirable character. A bit mad. Well you're not entirely wrong there. Though I don't bite heads off rats anymore. Not since I lost me teeth. But I know my job. I've had a good look around here. You've got problems and they're all furry and have four legs."

"I would expect you to say that, it's part of your sales pitch."

"How's about this for a sale's pitch? In a month it will be Easter and people will be pouring into your zoo. That's if they can find the space, because by that time, there will be more rats than people. And of course then it will be too late to do anything. Rats can breed every four weeks and every female rat will be working overtime to transform your zoo into the village of Hamlyn. Once you have an out of control plague of rats, the council will close you down. You won't be able to get a job in charge of a rabbit hutch.

"Good luck Mr Gaylord." The phrase closed down, focused my attention.

"I'll put you on a month's trial."

"Deal," Farley said. "But I want a zoo keeper's wage and 50p for every rat."

"How will I know how many rats you've killed?"

"I'll deliver them to your office. You pay me and you keep the rats. Oh and I'll need an office."

"What do you need an office for? "

Farley looked me up and down "You've got an office."

"I'm the zoo manager."

"I'm the rat catcher. I need an office to plan my strategies. And a place for Wayne and Stella."

I had visions of this character moving his entire family into the zoo.

"I'm sorry, I can't have children running around."

"Well don't have children running around, I'm talking Ferrets."

"Oh I see! I can perhaps let you have the use of the pump room under the aquarium. It's out of the way. The last thing I want is you tearing around the zoo catching rats in front of the public."

"No worries on that score. Stealth is my middle name. It's not by the way, it's Clarence, but you get my meaning."

Farley then grabbed my hand and shook it vigorously, while grinning and revealing two lonely black teeth.

"I really like you Gaylord." For a moment I felt uneasy, as he gazed into my face, winked and slowly pulled me towards him. I wrenched my hand free, trying to smile while examining an unidentifiable stain that had appeared in the middle of my palm.

I escorted our newly hired rat catcher, to the pump room in the labyrinth of tunnels under the aquarium complex. Here the generators were housed, that powered the pumps for the aquarium tanks. It was smelly, cold and damp, with the constant sound of dripping water. It was the kind of place that would give even Stephen King the creeps. Nobody would contemplate spending time here.

"This is just up my street Mr Gaylord. I always find the sound of running water very soothing. I'll move my stuff in tomorrow."

"Farley I'd appreciate it if you would call me Naylor?"

"No problem. So you'd prefer me to call you Naylor when we are in my office and Gaylord when we are in yours."

I ventured down to the pump room only the once. On opening the door a few inches, I saw Farley seated at a table scrutinising a pile of dead rats. Sorting through them with one hand.

That was stomach churning enough, but when I saw in his other hand he had a large sandwich, I closed my eyes and then the door. The heap of dead rats on the table was proof Farley was doing his job. But I had an uneasy feeling about him being on the premises and I still couldn't remove the stain from my hand.

The zoo rat population subsequently decreased dramatically. But every fortnight, Farley would appear at my office with a sack full of dead rats.

After emptying them on the office floor, he'd proceed to count them, commenting on the special features of each corpse. "Thirty two there Mr Gaylord. Mostly sewer rats. See all the scabs on their faces. Very prone to eczema and dermatitis when they live in sewers. It's all them foul gases that do it. We'd have scabs and eczema too if we lived in sewers Mr Gaylord. I think that's where I picked up these weeping sores on me stomach."

Farley wrenched up a perforated grey stained vest. "See!"

"Farley! Little busy right now. How much do I owe you?"

"Let's see. Including the delivery charge and sack allowance."

"Delivery charge! Sack allowance! You only walk a hundred yards to my office."

"Sacks ain't what they used to be Mr Gaylord, they wear out rapidly. I put it down to climate change."

I counted out the money and put it on the desk, avoiding contact with Farley's large stained hands, in case I acquired another unerasable stain."

Can't you tidy yourself up a bit, where's the uniform we gave you?"

"I only wear it on my days off, I find it keeps clean that way."

I opened the metal cash box and took out some money, Farley snatched it faster than a swooping seagull stealing a Cornish pasty. Then swung his sack over his shoulder, leaving the office singing.

As soon as the rat problem was dealt with, I wanted Farley off the premises.

I was hearing too many reports of his light fingered activities.

He regularly helped himself to the food intended for the animals. His excuse for twice falling through the skylight of the animal food store, was that he was hunting rats at night.

Just the other day, a keeper on the big cats had loaded his barrow up with meat, after turning his back for a moment, he found a large leg of beef had gone missing. Farley was seen leaving the scene briskly, with a large protuberance under his coat.

The same day an irate ostrich keeper burst into my office.

"Yesterday my female ostrich was sitting on ten eggs. Farley was seen hanging around. Now she's now just sitting on her bum."

Then there were the scams. The zoo no longer operated Elephant rides. But Jim Bedford the head keeper of Elephants, was regularly confronted with zoo visitors, complaining they had handed over money for an elephant ride, to a keeper wearing a tea shirt with 'Rat Terminator' emblazoned on the front.

Winter had come and gone. There were no rats to be seen. But every fortnight Farley delivered his sack of the rats to my office.

"It would be so much easier if you just put me on permanent celery Mr Gaylord."

"You will never ever be permanent Farley. When the rats go, so will you."

"As you will." Farley said collecting his money.

"It looks like we could be together for quite some time then."

As Farley walked out of the office. I watched him swagger off across the yard whistling, while I pondered on what he meant by, we could be together for quite a while.

A call from Jim Bedford the elephant keeper, was the beginning of the end for Farley.

"When are you going to get around to demolishing the old reptile house? Apart from it being a right eyesore, it's falling down."

Jim was a grade one moaner and the zoo union representative, who never failed to ring me at least once a day.

"I was taking Sheba for her early morning stroll around the zoo. She always likes to stop at the old reptile house and pull out weeds that are growing in the brickwork. This morning she nearly brought half of one wall down. That's a health and safety matter boss. I thought I might end up in one of those adverts, have you had an accident at work ? Well I nearly did."

"I'll look into that Jim. Leave it with me."

I was trying to get Jim off the phone, which was never easy.

"Do you know that Reptile House is alive with rats?

You can hear them squeaking from outside."

"Did you say rats?"

"It must be teeming with them. I've seen Farley in and out of there many a time. It's a wonder he doesn't do something about them." I smelled more than a rat. Opening the desk drawer I took out the keys to the old reptile house, then made my way over there.

As I unlocked the old heavy door of the dilapidated building, I could clearly hear rodents squeaking. When I saw what was inside, I knew what Farley meant by, we could be together for a long time. It was rat city. There were wire cages from floor to ceiling, containing rats of varying sizes, mothers with babies, colony cages. A clipboard on the wall recorded breeding details. It was obvious that Farley was industriously 'breeding' his salary.

When confronted, Farley as always had the last say.

"Mr Gaylord, Rats at your zoo are totally extinct. The rats in the reptile house were part of an experiment. Now that experiment is completed, I must resign to work on my book 'Rat Catching for Dummies.' And you Mr Gaylord, will be getting the first signed copy."

"Bye Farley."

The following year, I was speaking to a fellow zoo manager.

He happened to mention he'd just employed a rat catcher.

"The funny thing is, we never really thought we had a rat problem. But this chap turns up with a large ginger rat in a cage, he'd just caught outside my office. We hired him on the spot."

"Tell me Geoffrey, do you have an arrangement where you pay him for the dead rats he delivers to you?"

"How did you know?"

YOU'VE BEEN FRAMED

A neighbour Des was always quizzing me about birds he could breed that could make him rich. Following the Harry Potter films, depicting the Owlery at Hogwarts, there was a craze, thankfully short lived, for pet owls.

"Pet owls, now they seem to be a money spinner Bill. I suppose the ones that can talk would be the most valuable."

"Valuable and very rare Des."

"Let me run this idea by you Bill. Breeding parrots, the same colours as a national flag. The millennium is coming up soon, red, white and blue budgies. Surely they'd fly off the shelves. There's nobody can touch me as a breeder. Used to rear hundreds of koi carp.

Do parrots have any special requirements I should know about Bill?"

"As a rule of thumb Des, they all prefer to breed above water."

A discovery in a junkyard, convinced one young bird keeper called Derek he'd struck gold.

"I bet you've never seen one of these Bill," Derek said, beaming as he placed the badly mounted bird on the table.

"The market square is full of them Derek."

"It's a pigeon I agree. But a special one. See the name on the plaque, 'Martha,' you know what that means."

"At a guess, it was called Martha."

"This species is extinct."

"No Derek it's stuffed. And so were you if you paid a lot for it."

"I've done a background check. The north American passenger pigeon was once the most plentiful bird on the planet, flocks used to take days to fly overhead, but they were hunted to extinction. The last passenger pigeon died in Cincinnati Zoo in 1914 and here's the clincher, it was a hen bird and it was called Martha. When this has been to auction I might buy my own zoo."

"Derek! Passenger pigeons were slim like Mourning doves, or our Turtle dove, this is more like one of the hot dog munching doves that frequent Trafalgar Square."

"We'll see when it goes to auction. Even if it's not Martha, it's a passenger pigeon"

"Mounted passenger pigeons are uncommon, but not rare, as there were so many of them. But I know for certain this is not one."

"How can you be so sure?"

"Two reasons. Martha, the last passenger pigeon resides in the Smithsonian Institute in Washington DC. And secondly, your one eyed bird is wearing a racing ring."

Elephant birds, large flightless birds standing twelve feet high existed up until the 18th Century in Madagascar. Their eggs, the largest known bird eggs, sometimes measuring three feet in circumference, are owned by a handful of private collectors and exhibited by a few of the world's museums, including The British Natural History museum. Their rarity was highlighted in 2013 when one sold at Christies for over £66,000.

Visiting a flea market Derek came across an old wooden glass fronted cabinet that appeared to contain an elephant bird's egg. When Derek made enquires about the cabinet's contents, all the disinterested owner knew, it was simply listed as a giant egg.

Derek wasn't going to enlighten him. A deal was struck. Derek handed over £40. It was only when Derek struggled to lift the cabinet and the owner offered the use of his forklift to hoist the cabinet into the car boot. Did Derek realise, the elephant bird's egg he'd purchased was a concrete replica.

Derek was forever hoping to find that elusive lottery win antique and on one occasion did temporarily acquire one. He was forever buying up old bird paintings, hoping he'd discover one by John Gould or James Audubon.

His most recent purchase was an old dirt encrusted painting.

Etched on the back was the name Jean Cherin. As was his routine, Derek contacted an art dealer.

At the mention of Jean Cherin, the dealer became excited and heaped praise on this French master. But Derek as always didn't want details.

"Yes, yes, but is it valuable?"

"If it's a Cherin and in good condition. Yes it is."

When Derek showed me the painting, I thought it resembled a paint by numbers exercise, where the artist had got the numbers wrong.

"Unusual subject Derek, penguins in a tree."

"They're parrots. You can plainly see they're Parrots"

"At what stage in their evolution? Or would they be those type of parrots that shuffle along in the Antarctic snow and eat fish?" Derek was most offended.

"It's a highly collectable painting."

Derek stormed off, after I pointed out, the only way his painting would be collectable is if it was left alongside a wheely bin.

Derek was convinced he'd found a masterpiece. He had the awful painting cleaned and fitted in a new frame, disposing of the old garish frame. His meeting with the art dealer was brief. "I'm sorry, your painting of the penguins in a tree is not a Jean Cherin."

"But I saw his name, he painted it."

The art dealer laughed.

"Forgive me, but you see Jean Cherin wasn't a painter, he was an 18th Century picture frame maker and carver. If you get your hands on one of creations, you will have struck gold."

PARROT FASHION

Songbirds are natural mimics and often sample parts other birds' songs to add variety and improve their own. The Marsh Warbler is a maestro mimic, imitating an amazing 76 species of birds. When you hear him perform, he sounds as if he's invited lots of friends round.

The supreme mimic among birds, is the Australian Lyrebird. In addition to bird and animal calls, it can reproduce among other things, the sound of car alarms, chain saws and torrential rain. A resident lyrebird in an Australian national park, used to accurately imitate the sound of a flute. Research revealed, twenty years earlier, the daughter of a woodcutter living in the park, regularly sat on the veranda practising her flute.

A number of birds can mimic human speech. Including crows, jays, magpies and starlings. Even canaries and some other finches such as bullfinches, have been known to say a few words. The Indian Hill Mynah, a relative of the starling, reproduces human speech more accurately than any other bird. But parrots have the largest vocabularies and the ability to associate words and phrases. Using verbal labelling, the method a child uses when learning a language.

The problem with a parrot's ability to mimic, is their lack of discretion. Those family tiffs where insults are thrown about like confetti, then forgotten when peace resumes, are fodder for the parrot. Long after the hatchet has been buried, the parrot will dig it up and regularly remind you of every barbed jibe.

Hushed conversations and clandestine phone calls, overheard by the hooked beaked recorder, will also be noted and stored away. Then out of the blue repeated.

"Why don't you come round tonight, he's working late."

This is usually the point in the proceedings, when a parrot is swiftly re-homed. "The parrot!, I thought he would be better off in a zoo. Overseas."

Parrots often excel at abusive language and once learned, use it regularly. The reason being, taboo words or phrases are guaranteed to elicit an immediate response. It's not unknown for social gatherings to have erupted in mayhem and embarrassment. When the previously well behaved parrot, having secretly mastered Anglo-Saxon phrases, has loudly invited everybody to go forth and multiply.

Some parrots swear and say little else. I once met up with an old featherless cockatoo in a run down Sydney bar, whose only excuse for a crest were two bent feathers on his head. He was reputed to be a hundred years old. Which would explain the state of his body.

This resembled an oven ready chicken, left at the bottom of the freezer for decades. The naked cockatoo's vocabulary was limited to one phrase, striding up and down the bar and attempting to climb into customer's beer glasses, he would shout at ten minute intervals, "Where's my ******* feathers? "

Some zoos have a behind the scenes area, where ex-pet parrots habituated to shouting obscenities, can live out their days swearing at each other, but otherwise offending nobody else.

At Adelaide Zoo Australia, I was introduced to the biggest bunch of foul-mouthed cockatoos you could ever meet. They were housed in an off limits building, nicknamed 'Speaker's Corner.' I was assigned the task of feeding and cleaning them. Every time I set foot in the place, the air turned blue. And my nationality, gender and marriage of my parents was vigorously challenged.

Some of the bird's vocabularies consisted of nothing else but a long list of swear words and phrases of abuse. They'd run through their repertoire then start again.

One bird constantly uttered the phrase "Unwashed, pommie, commie, mongrel bastard," over and over again. But this sounded like a compliment, compared to what some of the other birds were calling me. They say you've never been properly insulted, until you've heard it from an Australian. I'd say, you've never been properly insulted, until you've heard it from a parrot, taught by an Australian.

Highly intelligent, parrots are demanding pets and unlike dogs, will happily bite the hand that feeds them.

Because larger parrots can live to be thirty, forty and even longer, some outliving their owners. (Cocky, a sulphur Crested Cockatoo at London zoo reached the age of 82)

Consequently, if you happen to be the member of your family who has been sworn in as parrot enemy number one. You can expect to be attacked in the comfort of your own home for the rest of your life.

Parrots sometimes take a dislike to certain people for no apparent reason. In the following case, it was based on sound judgement.

There was an unpopular zoo keeper called Melvin, who would ingratiate himself with anybody of influence. On the board of zoo trustees was an affluent hotel owner, who wanted somebody to care for Pluto, his beloved African Grey parrot, while he went into hospital. Melvin fell over himself rushing to volunteer. And Pluto set up home with Melvin.

Pluto was okay with most people, most people that is, apart from Melvin. Being a wild caught African Grey, he would growl when he saw someone or something he didn't like. When he as much as caught a glimpse of his young zoo keeper carer, his growls would rise in volume until they were ear piercing.

The old man's hospital visits increased and Pluto and Melvin spent increasingly more time together. Melvin was not enjoying the company of his new flat mate one bit. He suffered a barrage of bites every time he had to replenish food or clean Pluto's cage. And he was getting very little sleep, due to the continuous growling.

Melvin hung in there. The reason was not altruistic, the old man was at death's door and it was common knowledge he was not on the best of terms with his family.

Melvin was hoping in return for caring for Pluto, he would line his grimy little pockets. Pluto's owner passed away. Melvin was invited to the reading of his will. When the old man's family saw Melvin, he was met with icy stares. Melvin took this as a positive clue his windfall was imminent. It was. The family got nothing, the zoo got the old man's money and Melvin got Pluto.

Parrots have incredibly long memories. Phrases or words they have learned in their youth and have never spoken for years, will suddenly re-emerge, triggered by a person or event.

At one major British Zoo, there was a beautiful sulphur crested cockatoo, who was a brilliant talker. In the wild cockatoos are well known for their raucous screeching, used in communication with their colleagues. When flocks are feeding on the ground designated individuals act as sentries, taking up position high in nearby trees. When they sound their alarm call, it's deafening. But curiously, cockatoos who imitate human speech, usually have a high-pitched soft gentle voice, almost like that of a little girl.

This particular cockatoo would greet all comers with a friendly, "Hello my darling," or, "Kiss me quick." But occasionally would lapse into speaking in an unknown language. (I say he, because unlike females who have nut-brown eyes, he had deep red eyes). The bird had been donated to the zoo, by a well-travelled merchant seaman over twenty years ago. Other than that his history was unknown.

Zoos try to avoid housing birds singly and pair them up as soon as possible.

This is not always easy. One might think parrots who often mate for life and have strong pair bonds, would be overjoyed to be presented with a mate. But some parrots, especially male cockatoos, regularly turn up their beak at an arranged marriage and become so aggressive, the female has to be removed.

However, the male cockatoo in question was soon paired up with a compatible mate. The minute he saw her, his chest puffed out, his crest shot up and he was smitten.

What happened, as so often does in this situation, the male bird stopped talking. One theory why Parrots imitate human speech, is that they see humans as surrogate mates. This would explain why male parrots are often more receptive to women and vice-versa, the so called ' cross over theory.'

At the zoo where the cockatoo lived, there was an international meeting of zoo directors. All the animal houses were spruced up and the whole zoo smelled strongly of paint. A directive went out to all staff to get their hair cut and wear full uniforms.

Eccentric keepers, of which there were more than a few, would be given tasks behind the scenes, to avoid them confronting the directors and telling them all their troubles.

On the day of the conference, the zoo directors had enjoyed a well-lubricated lunch and were all relaxed, perhaps seeing double, but all in a jovial mood. It was then time for a leisurely stroll around the zoo, with our boss leading the way. He was on good form, swapping pleasantries, joking occasionally, but with restraint. Very much aware that where there is a language barrier, joking can backfire. Recently in a speech to a group of Japanese zoo directors, he had enquired if their large mammals had mated successfully that year. What he had actually said, in his limited grasp of Japanese,

"Have all your wives successfully mated this year?"

Our director and his party, stopped at the aviary of a female Amazon parrot called Dr Dolittle. She was renowned for her rendition of, "Talk to the animals," delivered in a high-pitched soprano voice. With an audience in attendance the Amazon launched into her party piece with relish. All the visiting directors were greatly amused and applauded appreciatively.

The group moved on, only pausing momentarily at the aviary which housed the sulphur-crested cockatoos, who were busy preening each other and unimpressed by the eminent visitors. But the Russian director, a parrot enthusiast, stopped to admire them. With his shaven head, rotund shape and tight fitting suit, he closely resembled one of those little plastic men you might see at the bottom of a budgie cage.

"Hallo pretty birdie!" he called out in Russian.

The male cockatoo, recognising a familiar accent, raised his crest, bobbed his head up and down and replied in Russian, followed by a cackle.

The smile immediately fell from the Russian director's face.

144

He stared at the cockatoo in disbelief and spoke again in Russian. This time in a stern tone, "Hallo…birdie!" The bird again repeated its original reply, followed by a raucous laugh.

This incensed the Russian director so much, he thumped on the aviary wire with his fists. The cockatoo laughed all the more, repeating the offending phrase over and over.

The red-faced Russian gripped the aviary wire, shaking it furiously, giving the impression to any onlooker he was being electrocuted.

The cockatoo repeated the offending phrase, with additional ones he'd just remembered. The zoo director sweating profusely, his head turning red from the neck up, looked as if it would explode if put under further pressure. And further pressure was imminent. The bilingual cockatoo was just getting into his stride. He marched proudly up and down his perch rattling off a monologue. Which, judging by the behaviour of the Russian director, who was now collecting gravel from the path to throw at the cockatoos, was nothing short of the mother of all insults.

The cockatoo was completely unperturbed by the shower of stones and treated it as a congratulatory gesture, similar to when roses are thrown to opera singers.

Hanging from his branch, with wings outstretched, he demonstrated he was also capable of shouting Russian insults whilst upside down.

The other zoo directors some distance ahead, were puzzled when they looked back to see, the Russian director enthusiastically throwing gravel at the cockatoo aviary. Suspecting the cause of this bizarre behaviour was connected to the contents of a vodka bottle, they ran to restrain him. Grabbing his arms they held him with his back to the aviary. The human fracas excited the cockatoos so much, they flew on the wire, screeching excitedly and began pecking at the soviet director through the wire. The victim replied in Russian, the equivalent of:

"My buttocks are being chewed by cockatoos." The other directors not having come across this in their phrase books, continued restraining him against the wire.

Our director realising that his soviet colleague was being assaulted, wrenched him away from the aviary. Then attempted to pacify him, by placing his hands on the shaking soviet's shoulders.

The Russian director pushed our boss's hands away and started jumping up and down. The other directors gasped in astonishment. Everybody wanted to get a better view of what was going on. Within seconds, there were half a dozen keepers industriously sweeping the small area in front of the cockatoo's aviary. The red-faced little Russian, tired of jumping, breathlessly rounded on our boss.

"It's not amusements, not funnies, to teach parrot anti-soviet slogans. You made me laughing stick. Why you do this? Are you so jealous of Moscow Zoo because it makes your zoo look like, like a market pet shop?" Our director's short fuse was ablaze. He leaned his head back skywards and gave out one short sarcastic laugh.

"Jealous! Now that is a joke. Moscow Zoo is glum, gloomy, grey and miserable, like the people who work there. Who could be jealous of that? And by the way Leo, why can't you ever get a suit in your size?"

The international zoo director's meeting was a rip-roaring failure. A bilingual cockatoo had succeeded in putting international zoo relations back twenty years.

HANK AND WILMA'S AVIARY

Landscaping zoo animal accommodation has reached a level of art in some zoos. The German zoos were the original innovators and their naturalistic approach of landscaping to simulate animal habitats, has been copied and perfected by many major zoos, especially in the USA. Now birds and animals are often routinely exhibited in replicas of their natural habitats, sometimes temperature-controlled.

A far cry from sterile concreted cages and tree-less aviaries found in most zoos within living memory.

Having been involved in bird keeping, (aviculture) for many years I have seen some aviaries where the birds looked so embarrassed; they didn't know where to put their beaks.

The worse exhibit I ever saw was so bad the photos I took refused to allow themselves to be developed. The aviary was called the 'South American Vulture Aviary.' Unique, in that it didn't contain vultures. The aviary housed Vulturine Guinea fowl, the bald headed variety of guinea fowl, with tasselled neck plumes. They shared the aviary with a pair of Crested Caracaras, long legged, South American hawks. Who spend a great deal of time on the ground feeding on carrion and unlike most species of falcons, adjust well to aviary life. These were both attractive interesting species, but the aviary was eye catching for the wrong reasons.

The perches were red and white-banded poles designed for a horse jump. And a large ceramic bath, complete with taps, was sunk in the ground to provide water.

As if that wasn't distasteful enough, the zoo owner had hung a plastic human skeleton in one corner, with the sign round its neck.

"Don't feed the vultures, I did and look what happened."

How not to landscape an aviary was emphasised when I met an American couple I'll call Hank and Wilma. They'd read an article of mine in a bird magazine and made contact.

"As a world expert on birds, you're invited to inspect our newly completed aviary."

I checked the name and address on the envelope. It was mine. Seems like the world expert was busy and they had invited me in instead.

Arriving at Hank and Wilma's house the doorbell gave me an indication of what was in store, as it blasted out the theme to the film 'Born Free'. Getting no answer at the door, I proceeded along a side alley. You could not miss the aviary.

The sign 'The Aviary' circled in coloured lights, wouldn't have looked out of place as a billboard on the LA freeway.

The backdrop of the flight was adorned with colourful murals, depicting palm trees, smiling crocodiles, miserable monkeys and parrots of every inconceivable colour. Bunches of plastic bananas and grapes, hung from the painted branches.

Birds would have had no problems finding the amenities. There were signposts everywhere: 'Drinks this way,' 'Queue here for bird seed.'

And my favourite, 'Strictly no migrating.'

Hank and Wilma appeared wearing ultra large kaftans, depicting species of birds, (all nine thousand it seemed.) The man in a thick Bronx accent yelled:

"Bill! my man." The woman screamed and hurled herself at me yelling,

"Bird brother! When I breathlessly surfaced from the folds of her kaftan, she waved her hand towards the aviary.

"All the murals are my work Bill." She was obviously from the school of art, that dictates, when in doubt which colour to choose, use all of them.

Hank clamped a large arm around by shoulders, pulling my head onto his shoulder.

And commenced patting my cheek

"I just don't know where she gets it Bill." I wanted to say, "Find out Hank and cut off her supply."

Unable to escape I was sandwiched by kaftans.

Hank cupped his ear, "Wilma! I think I feel a jungle effect coming on." then pointed a remote control...

A recording of Hank's voice boomed out from speakers on top of the aviary.

"You think you're in England. No way, you're deep in the Amazonian jungle."

Hank enthusiastically went into his beat box routine, as a cacophony of wildlife noises kicked in, including kookaburras, parrots, wolves and owls. With Tarzan, cheetah and David Attenborough on backing vocals. We all swayed to the lack of rhythm. The cacophony ended with what else? A cuckoo and a lion's roar.

"Wilma and I mixed the music ourselves. So what do you think of our aviary Bill? You can be honest. Give it to us like it is."

I smiled, swallowed and lied big time.

"Unusual. It's a pity more people don't vandalise, I mean design, an aviary with such individual style. By the way, what kind of birds do you intend keeping?"

Hank grabbed Wilma's hand for support and then subjected me to more cheek patting.

"You know little buddy, it's been a hard decision. But we've decided, we don't really need birds, they'd just kinda spoil it. Now! Let's all hug and bless the aviary."

UNDER NEW MANAGEMENT

It was obvious when I attended the interview the zoo was in decline. Derek the owner hadn't a clue.

"The penguins don't look in good condition Derek, what do you feed them on?"

"If I remember rightly, I think we feed them on a Wednesday."

Some of the animals were so old, they were at an earlier stage in their evolution. But I took the job, because Derek sold me the vision of new enclosures, aviaries stocked with birds of my choice. In truth he wanted somebody to maintain the collection till he could find a gullible buyer. As the months passed, an increasingly despondent Derek admitted if no buyer was forthcoming he would have to close.

One morning Derek bounded into the food prep room almost doing handstands.

"Good news, I've saved the zoo. The new owner Mrs Rotherhyde will meet up with you all presently."

"What do you know about the new owner Derek."

"Only that she has lots of money and she's deranged."

"How do you know she's deranged?"

"It's obvious, she bought this place. Good luck"

Lady Rotherhyde's meek exterior hid a steely determination.

"Being in charge of the zoo Bill, you must blame yourself for it's lack of success."

"I do feel partly responsibility."

"Nonsense, you're totally responsible. So I'll give you a short time to turn it around, before I consider replacing you. I don't know anything about zoos but I know about business. We must become more commercial and family orientated. I'm building a kiddies playground. Each of you will take it in turns to dress up in an animal costume, you can choose which species."

"Oh thankyou."

"Then you will meet and greet visitors at the entrance with trays of sweets." This brought protests from the motley crew of keepers.

"I'm a zoo keeper not a cartoon character."

"Your choice," Mrs Rotherhyde pointed out.

"A cartoon character or an ex zoo keeper. And when you're not in bird costumes I want you in your uniform. As it is, nobody knows you work here. And going by the length of the meal and tea breaks, some of you hardly do. I've designed some uniforms, but I can't remember whether they are maroon or royal blue. Anyway, your names are on the front. Our sponsors names are on the back."

"Sponsors! We are zoo keepers not mobile placards."

"Funds have to be generated to pay your wages and run the zoo."

The uniforms arrived and were unique. Red trousers and blue shirt. Like the others mine had my name printed on the front of the shirt:

"Hi I'm Bill."

On the back in larger print was 'Thompkins High Class Butchers' and 'Parkinson's Funeral Directors.' Visitor numbers increased and the uniforms did encourage the visitors to ask questions, but they were usually enquiries about pies, or funeral arrangements.

Despite badgering Mrs Rotherhyde to buy more animals and birds, she was adamant more visitors had to flow through the turnstiles and generate revenue first. I argued that at least the enclosures and aviaries should be improved. The penguin pond for instance, had been designed by Derek. Ignorant of a penguin's needs, it was furnished with perches and nest boxes.

Mrs Rotherhyde agreed an upgrade of the most run down aviaries and animal enclosures. But she was adamant the zoo stock would not increase till visitors did.

"I think we have enough animals and birds for the moment and anyway the replica animals and birds are cheaper to maintain. I like cartoon characters birds like Daffy duck and Roadrunner. I would like to see more of those in the aviaries."

"Are we a zoo or Disneyland Mrs Rotherhyde?"

"We are a zoo, but if that becomes a problem to me, it will quickly cease to be a zoo. And then I wouldn't require any zoo keepers would I? Attract more visitors and you can buy more birds and animals. Get on with it!"

Reluctantly I did. The animal's tea party and subsequent food fight was a great success. It drew a big crowd and was covered by the local press. The only downside for me was when the press photographer removed the head from my daffy duck costume.

The zoo was now a popular venue showing a healthy profit. But I was still at loggerheads with Mrs Rotherhyde.

She had the weirdest ideas about running a zoo. Sometimes I didn't know if she was joking.

"Bill I've a great idea for Christmas. Knitted body warmers for the larger birds.

I can just see the ostriches and penguins wearing them."

"In the name of zoology there is no way birds in this zoo are wearing knitted body warmers."

"Visitor numbers have increased over the past month. I've endorsed what I think you will agree is a generous budget to buy birds and animals."

"In that case, I'll go and get the penguins' measurements."

THE BEAST OF WARRENDALE

The abundance of small zoos in the UK, in the late sixties and seventies, meant there was fierce competition in enticing visitors through their turnstiles.

At the time, safari parks were one of the new innovations in exhibiting zoo animals. Debt ridden aristocrats down to their last butler, turned over their grounds to free range exotic animals. Giraffes and other wild animals strolled around the grounds of stately homes. For as little as a pound you could drive among big game animals, soaking up the simulated safari atmosphere. While baboons demonstrated their skills at dismantling your moving car. Unlike African game parks, the animals could not retreat from the humans in their midst. Safari Parks were very much an experiment. Nobody really knew how the animals would react to humans driving among them. They might treat them as meals on wheels. Fortunately as it turned out, they were largely disinterested.

Many zoo owners in the competitive cut throat times, were larger than life characters, who stretched their entrepreneurial skills to the limit. Others were out and out criminals.

I was once hired to run a new zoo by two businessmen brothers. It transpired they were conmen, probably thrown out of the mafia for being too ruthless. Their zoo was full of potential, so I thought. The zoo buildings and enclosures were half finished, but there were no animals or birds. These were supposed to be acquired when the building work was completed.

Once installed as a zoo manager, I found that the zoo was a money laundering operation. It was never going to be finished. I was running a zoo with no animals or keepers. Nor was I getting my full pay till the zoo opened.

When I resigned, the zoo owners threatened to sue me. Claiming due to my actions, the zoo had been forced to close. Although it had never been open in the first place.

Another zoo boss and self-styled entrepreneur I crossed paths with, was Reg Flowers. Before becoming an incompetent zoo director, Reg was an incompetent zoo keeper, who rose in the ranks after a run in with porcupines.

Contrary to belief, porcupines don't shoot their spines, they simply relax muscles and loosen them. They then either reverse into you with spines erect. Or when being chased by an enemy, stop abruptly with spines erect and the pursuer gets the point. You could say, a whole lot of points. It's a highly efficient means of defence.

Man eating tigers when shot and examined, often have broken porcupine quills embedded in various parts of their body, usually the paws, making it difficult for them to chase their usual prey. The reason it's believed, they switched to the easy hunting option of killing humans.

Reg had collided with the porcupines while sweeping their enclosure and had acquired two buttocks worth of spines. Because the porcupines couldn't be locked away during cleaning. Reg sued the zoo for failing to provide a safe working environment. When Reg demonstrated to his lawyer how his accident happened, he collected even more spines than he did in the original incident. But he won his case and a hefty settlement.

Reg always had more money than sense, now he had enough to cause real mayhem and bought his own zoo. He chose a scenic location in the wilds of the English Lake District. To protect the innocent and not annoy the guilty, let's call the location Warrendale.

Unfortunately the zoo was almost inaccessible, but it had an ancient public right of way running through it.

Consequently most visitors consisted of lost country walkers, who stumbled upon the zoo, wearing worn out boots, clutching torn maps.

Reg tried to publicise the zoo and attract visitors, by using the power of the local press. Whenever a news item about the zoo appeared in 'The Warrendale Gazette,' visitors increased.

Reg, a natural showman, would position himself at the zoo entrance, under the sign, 'Animel Heven.' (the work of Theo, a dyslexic sign writer.) Here with a talking parrot on his arm and a snake draped around his neck, he would welcome visitors.

But once inside, they found there was little to see.

Reg had spent most of his money building animal accommodation and had little money left to buy animals. He got round this problem by placing signs on vacant enclosures:

"Away filming with David Attenborough", or "Animals Hibernating."

In autumn and winter the zoo was empty. But like all zoos, the bills for the animal food, heating and keepers wages still had to be met.

One winter, when the zoo turnstile was in danger of rusting up from lack of use and the stack of bills on Reg's desk was blocking out the light. Reg sent photos of zoo animals in picturesque winter settings to the Gazette. The only problem was, the zoo animals in the photos didn't actually live at Reg's zoo. The ruse encouraged visitors to brave the inclement Lake District weather and visit 'Animel Heven.'

But one visitor, a local councillor, complained he had visited the zoo. But was unable to find the penguins or their woolly feathered youngsters depicted in the Gazette.

The Gazette editor quizzed Reg, who announced his beloved penguins had regrettably escaped. This got him off the hook with the Gazette, but straight into hot water with the RSPCA. They demanded to know, how penguins who walk like contestants in a sack race, could possibly tunnel out of their enclosure as Reg had claimed and go on tour, shuffling around the Lake District.

Reg had to act fast and cover his tracks. He simultaneously contacted the RSPCA and the Gazette, telling them the penguins had been recaptured, then announced:

"But regrettably, because they are such little Houdinis. I can't guarantee they will not escape again. So I've decided, it's in the penguin's best interests, to re-home them in another zoo, abroad."

The episode damaged what little credibility Reg had with the Gazette. The zoo's lifeline was publicity and now it seemed he had lost local news coverage, but not for long.

A beaver called Toby went AWOL from his enclosure, on a trial separation from his mate Olive. Travelling overland Toby discovered the lake of his dreams, setting up camp in the grounds of a private estate.

Toby had been out of the zoo for three weeks and it might seem strange that nobody missed him. But beavers are shy secretive creatures. Often the only sign of their presence, or rather their departure, is their warning to other beavers. Which is the loud slap of their round flat tail on the surface of the water, as they dive from view.

Nobody realised Toby has arrived in his new home, until he started demonstrating his lumberjack skills on a large group of weeping willows. Beavers love willows, young succulent twigs are stored for winter food, the mature trees with their soft wood are easily felled and branches used for dam building. Some of these branches take root and the dams become permanent fixtures. Which have altered the inland water way system, in parts of the world where beavers occur.

Toby worked like a beaver, toppling trees, constructing one dam after another. And commenced building a 'lodge', his living quarters, in the middle of the lake. This was constructed out of logs, plastered with mud and allowed to dry hard like cement. Under beaver building specifications, the entrance to a beaver's 'lodge' must always be under water. Toby achieved this by damming the outflow to the lake.

This raised the level of water, but also flooded nearby herbaceous borders, shrub beds and a tennis court. The owner of the estate was predictably unappreciative of Toby's landscaping skills. When he found out he had a beaver in residence he called Reg.

"How do you know it's our beaver?" Reg said. "It could be a wild one."

"According to my enquiries, beavers became extinct in this

country in the 16th century." Reg played the outside chance. "Perhaps one survived, in your lake. The one they missed."

"Mr Flowers, the grounds of my house once beautifully landscaped, now look like the everglades. If you do not take steps to remove this furry chainsaw. I will commence legal action."

The threat of being sued prompted Reg to draft in Olive, the female beaver, as a honey trap. As soon as Toby saw Olive's brown hairy face and prominent orange stained teeth, he couldn't help himself. Who could? He promptly surrendered.

Toby and Olive were reunited back at 'Animel Heven.' But the pair kick started Beavermania. The Gazette was reluctant to give Reg's zoo any more publicity. But public interest demanded they run a story about the escaped beaver. It wasn't a one off either. In newspaper parlance the story had legs. Readers were intrigued that an animal could transform an area simply by damming streams. The estate owner set himself up as the bad guy and went on record saying he wish he could have shot the beaver. Angry letters appeared in the paper, echoing the view that the beaver was behaving naturally and the estate owner was behaving abominably.

Some local residents confused the beaver with an otter and wrote irate letters reprimanding the estate owner for persecuting such a charming animal, whose only crime was to eat a few fish. It was all welcome publicity for the zoo. Visitors poured into 'Animel Heven' just to see the beavers. Reg commissioned Theo the sign writer, to put up a large sign depicting the dam making skills of 'Beevures.' Even the national press did a story on Toby and Olive.

The increase in revenue, meant for a couple of months, Reg was smoking cigars and basking in the publicity. But all things must pass and Beavermania eventually waned. Theo took his sign down in lieu of payment and Reg went back to borrowing cigarettes. But Beavermania had convinced Reg, escaped animals were the key to spinning turnstiles and he immediately started rigging escapes. But the escapes became so frequent, every morning animals waited at the gate of their enclosures in case it was their turn for an away day.

At first the Gazette covered every escape and recapture, even though they suspected the stunts were rigged. Reg as usual indulged in over kill. The same animals were repeatedly escaping and were always recaptured on the farm land of Reg's friend Simon.

The Gazette, so starved of news, it ran front page headlines such as, "Hat found in high street", eventually refused to print anymore zoo escape stories. The local council voiced their concerns about the abundance of escapes and threatened to close Reg down.

Around this time, The Dangerous Animals Act (1976) was passed. This meant private individuals and zoos could only keep big cats, monkeys and large or venomous snakes etc, if they had a licence. Which was only granted, following a rigorous zoo inspection.

Because of the Act, many private zoos closed. And there is suspicion, though never verified, that some private keepers of big cats, irresponsibly released them in the neighbouring countryside, rather than have them destroyed.

Over the years, unconfirmed sightings of wild cats have fuelled such legends as the, "The Beast of Bodmin," and, "The Beast of Exmoor." Reg was now about to create the Beast of Warrendale.

Pumas, also called Panthers, or Mountain Lions, are the most easily tamed of all the big cats. Reg acquired a silly tame Puma called Malcolm. Who would bound up to you, lie down and roll over, inviting you to tickle his belly. He was totally imprinted on humans and when he was in a romantic mood, would attempt to mate with a trouser leg, preferably corduroy.

Over the next couple of weeks, Reg coerced his keepers to anonymously phone the Gazette and report sightings of a large cat. The Gazette contacted Reg, enquiring if any of his big cats had escaped. Reg explained he didn't keep big cats at the zoo. But took the opportunity to stir rumours about a big cat living wild in Warrendale. Reg's plan was to increase the amount of bogus sightings, then announce he had captured the Beast of Warrendale. Malcolm would be put on display at 'Animel Heven,' and the turnstiles would spin ad infinitum. The plan was on track, until Malcolm went AWOL.

Twenty four hours later, Reg got a phone call from his friend Simon.

"I've got a mountain lion shut in my barn, I thought it would be yours."

"Simon you're a gem."

"And I've phoned the Gazette."

"Oh you haven't."

"But I always phone the Gazette when you have an escape."

Reg hurried over to Simon's farm but he was too late. Reporters and photographers had encircled the barn. When the barn doors were opened, Malcolm made a bee-line for Reg. The excitement of seeing Reg and the fact that he was wearing corduroy trousers, prompted Malcolm to enthusiastically display great affection. Cursing Reg, the press men climbed into their vehicles and departed.

The zoo limped along, as Reg sold off more animals to cover debts. A local sheep farmer bought the grazing rights to the entire zoo grounds. So unless you liked sheep, there wasn't a lot to see. Keepers in the past, subsisting on the meagre intermittent wages, often had to share food with the zoo inmates. But with most of the animals gone, the stark choice was now to leave or starve to death. Most of the keepers chose survival. Zoo closure loomed on the horizon, but Reg hoped even in the eleventh hour, he could somehow launch a plan that would save the zoo.

"I've a great idea to bring punters flocking in," said Reg slapping me on the shoulder. "I don't know why I never thought of it before. Dodos!"

"Dodos Reg?"

"Yes dodos." Reg said impatiently.

"Reg, dodos have been extinct since the seventeenth century."

"I know, that's the beauty of the plan. What an attraction. Imagine the press release; On show, the last dodo in captivity. We could get Theo to do us a sign, even he should be able to spell dodo."

I thought Reg had flipped.

"Reg, how can you exhibit a dodo, when dodo's are extinct, finoto, not around anymore? There's a certain problem with scarcity of supply"

"Doesn't matter, nobody will see it. We will have a bogus zoo visitor positioned at the front of its enclosure. When other visitors enquire, where's the dodo, our bogus visitor will explain. Dee dee the dodo ! Oh you've just missed her. She's waddled off inside. Wait for it, to tend to her eggs. See how this is panning out Bill. We are breeding dodos to release back in the wild. We will be the toast of the zoo world. Gerald Durrell will be green with envy. We could win an award, it deserves an award. What do you think?"

I lied, big time. "Could work I suppose."

If Reg's zoo was a ship, it would have been called Titanic II.

I wished him well and left for pastures new. Life for a time would seem dull after working at' Animel Heven,' but my life expectancy would increase.

The dodo was a fitting choice for Reg's last hair brained scheme. A month later 'Animel Heven' closed. And Reg accompanied the famous doomed bird, down the one way road to extinction. In the Gazette there appeared a short paragraph about the zoo closure. Ironically, it was the only authentic story regarding the zoo the paper had ever printed

BEGINNINGS:
THE BIRD NESTING GANG

In the late fifties and early sixties, children were usually only indoors when they were sick, being punished, or awaiting the arrival of the dreaded relatives. The natural history section of the local library, was the only indoor haunt I voluntarily frequented. There I would read up on the wildlife I discovered in the surrounding countryside, or learn about the exotic species in the local pet store. The latter was an Aladdin's cave of bubbling fish tanks, talking parrots, snakes, lizards and a mynah bird with a superior Scot's accent to the Scottish pet store owner.

In summer at the local library, a group of grubby kneed boys, myself included, regularly took two hefty volumes from the medical section, before disappearing among the labyrinth of tall shelves.

The head librarian once summoned us to his office and demanded to know why we were looking at medical dictionaries. The suspicion was, we were perusing pictures of human anatomy for non medical reasons. We explained, we required two large books to stand on in the natural history section, in order to reach the books on bird eggs.

Bird nesting was the main occupation of country boys in those days. The disturbance of bird's nests and the taking of bird's eggs, is now of course unacceptable and illegal. But fifty years ago bird nesting was common. But some did settle for variations of the hobby. Woodbine, a chain-smoking ginger haired boy, had a collection of over 300 eggs, in shoeboxes, all correctly labelled.

These would have been the envy of any bird nester, had they not all originated from his uncle's pigeon loft.

Boys who had the uncanny knack of finding bird's nests were held in high esteem.

An older boy nicknamed Tracker possessed this ability, even being able to find the eggs of the cuckoo. Highly prized by bird nesters, cuckoo's eggs often resemble the eggs of the owner of the nest in which the cuckoo lays her egg. Tracker was also a brilliant tree climber which explains why he often went barefoot. In his back pocket he carried a dog eared coverless copy of the bird nesters bible, the 'Observers Book of Bird Eggs'. Consequently when he told us he was an official bird nester working for the government, we believed him. Tracker collected eggs to order and traded us these for items we borrowed permanently from our parents.

To preserve a bird's egg, a hole had to be made in each end usually with a thorn. The egg was then put to the lips and the contents blown out.

Blowing an egg and discovering it was bad, was an occupational hazard of bird nesting. A bad egg would usually explode leaving the blower dazed and shaken. Smelling slightly worse than young boys did, at a time when only visible areas such as the face, hands and knees were regularly washed. After blowing a bad egg, it was always a race to the nearest stream. As it was common knowledge, if you didn't gargle with running water, you only had two minutes to live.

It was rumoured the only other antidote was swallowing frog spawn. Woodbine swore by this. But then Woodbine would swallow anything simply to boast.

Throughout the summer, our bird nesting gang of boys and girls, trekked over hill and dale, led by Tracker and accompanied by any dog that cared to tag along. Every aspect of nature was new and fascinating. Lifting stones and logs would reveal toads and grass snakes. When discovered, grass snakes would play dead lying on their backs with their tongues hanging out.

But when turned over, their deception was revealed. As they quickly flipped over on their backs again, sticking their tongue out. The girls collected armfuls of wild flowers and spent most of the day being plagued by bees. Tracker was so knowledgeable, he warned us against waving at aeroplanes, in case they mistook us for air traffic controllers and tried to land. We always seemed to be walking in areas where grass came up to our chins and on encountering livestock, it usually ended up like the Palermo Bull Run.

Country lanes in mid summer, heaved with wild flowers in a myriad of colours. The songbird chorus was deafening. Linnets with blood stained breasts and shiny golden yellow hammers seemed to sing from every hedge top. Barns and cowsheds were alive with swallows. When you entered you had to duck to avoid them, as they shot out like arrows. Buzzards seemed like giant eagles. Creamy plumaged Barn Owls, flying silently at dusk, were known as ghost owls.

Tawny Owls were notorious for dive-bombing anyone in the vicinity of their nest. Occasionally Tracker would spot a Golden Eagle circling high in the sky. He said these majestic birds carried off small children by the ears. Shoes and school caps often being found neatly stacked near their nests.

As a precaution, in 'eagle country,' we wore hats pulled down to ear lobe level. Except for Woodbine, who had a World War 2 soldier's tin helmet. In stormy weather Woodbine voluntarily walked ahead of the rest of us, in case his metal helmet was struck by lightening. He was always boasting his helmet could easily withstand a lightening bolt.

"It's British Army issue, I wouldn't even feel it."

Years earlier, a tractor driver who was working too close to a tree where a tawny owl was nesting, had been attacked by one of the nesting birds. In an effort to escape, he had sped off over hilly terrain and overturned the tractor, subsequently dying from his injuries. Tracker told us on moonlit nights, a tractor engine could be heard. As the headless driver haunted the fields, with his faithful headless sheep dog.

Tramping home as the sun went down, the girls clutching wilted flowers. Bird's eggs stuffed down a collection of socks all bird nesters carried. Frogspawn and newts in jam jars and grass snakes and slow worms in knotted sleeves of jumpers. The headless tractor driver would invariably come up in conversation. Then the pace would change from a walk to a tearful jog.

One day Tracker appeared, wearing shoes, stain free clothes, his hair flattened to his skull, generally looking pale. The suspicion was he'd had a bath. He explained he'd had to resign as official government bird nester and couldn't bird nest with us anymore.

Great times don't last forever. Tracker had discovered girls.

We suddenly realised we were teenagers; Grubby knees weren't fashionable anymore. It was time for members of the bird nesting gang to either grow breasts or spots and practise being miserable.

But I had to put my teenage angst on the back burner. I had a menagerie to care for. It was actually miscellaneous exotica from the local pet shop and wild hand reared, or rehabilitated injured birds and animals. But my dad referred to it as a menagerie.

"That bloody menagerie" to give it its full title.

RAISING HANK

The first wild bird I hand reared was a Tawny Owl.

"We have a round bird without any feet," the owl rescuers explained.

The feet were hidden but intact. The owlet was a ball of fluff not much bigger than a coconut, with a black beak, which it clicked repeatedly as a warning.

Its most impressive characteristic, that all owls possess, was a 14 neck vertebrae, enabling it to turn its head 270 degrees. Owls need to do this, as unlike other birds, their eyes are fixed in their sockets. This gave rise to the old superstition, if you keep circling an owl, it will follow you with its stare until its head falls off. My ultra-inquisitive neighbour took great interest in my menagerie.

"What have you got now?"

"A young Tawny Owl Mr Radcliffe? "

"That's never an owl. It's too fluffy."

Mr Radcliffe was never in agreement with my identification of wildlife. In a large tank I had slow worms. The shiny bronze coloured serpent-like British legless lizard. Mr Radcliffe's verdict:

"They're far too fast to be slow worms."

On questioning the owl rescuers, I learned the owl had been found in long grass. Owlets may leave the nest before they can fly properly, but parents know where they are and feed and care for them. Unfortunately, picking up fledgling birds on the assumption they are orphaned is irreversible. I now had the task of providing meat and roughage for this ball of fluff. The roughage is essential, as owls and other birds of prey, as well as some other birds like kingfishers and herons, following a meal, regurgitate bones, fur and feathers, in the form of pellets.

I rolled mincemeat mixed with chopped up chicken feathers into sausage shapes. Hank, as be became known, was named after Hank Marvin of the Shadows. Mainly because he looked as if he was wearing large glasses and being unsteady on his feet, I assumed he would be just as bad at dancing as the Shadowy Hank.

There was certainly nothing wrong with his appetite. He would swallow the chicken feather sausages in quick succession, then blink at an ever increasing rate before falling asleep.

Mr Radcliffe accosted me with a large book.

"I told you that bird is definitely not an owl. Look at page 32."

The Bumper book of Birds did not change my view of Hank's identity. The illustration depicted a juvenile emperor penguin.

"That's a three foot penguin Mr Radcliffe, a bit of rarity in the lake district woods."

Still unconvinced, Mr Radcliffe left embracing his book, muttering, "No way is that an owl."

The dog meat and chicken feathers, lacked the minerals that would be present in the skeleton of rodents. In Mr Radcliffe's opinion, feeding Hank meat and chicken feathers, would either cause him to chase hens, or spend time loitering outside butcher's shops when he grew up. Consequently I went small game hunting. Jam jars sunk in the garden flowerbeds, trapped field mice, voles and shrews. Being his natural diet. Hank relished these. Tawny Owls also eat larger insects. Being late summer, I found leaving the kitchen light on and the window open, cockchafer beetles sounding like rusty helicopters would fly in. Hank ate these, but regarded them as starters to his meal of mice.

Burying jam jars in the rose bed and encouraging night flying beetles, alarmed my parents. Who were torn between consulting a psychiatrist and adoption.

Hank escaped a number of times while exercising his wings. Much to the consternation of a local pigeon fancier. When the pigeons spotted Hank, they dispersed far and wide at great speed, the instinctive response to evading capture from a bird of prey. As pigeons are faster than bird's of prey and can only be caught by them when ambushed.

The pigeon fancier was livid. "I don't want you falconeering that owl near my pigeons again." Mr Radcliffe sprung to my defence.

"But it's not an owl."

A host of children myself included, would pursue Hank when he went AWOL. The film "Kes" was in cinemas at the time.

Ken Loach's iconic film of a boy's passion for a young kestrel.

I pondered if "Hank" the movie, would similarly captivate cinema audiences, winning me fame and fortune. Hank's fluffy down was gradually replaced by dappled mottled feathers. Appropriate camouflaged plumage for a woodland bird. On returning from holiday, Mr Radcliffe saw Hank in his adult garb for the first time.

"Still not convinced he's an owl Mr Radcliffe?"

"You don't expect me to believe that's the same bird do you?"

A phone call to the local zoo, persuaded me Hank was too tame to be released into the wild and would be better off in a zoo or bird garden.

THE NOBLE ART OF FLY BREEDING

In addition to hand rearing Hank, I also fostered foxes, badgers, hares and others. As well as a host of exotic animals. My zoo activities never went down too well with the neighbours. I once tried to breed maggots for my lizards and tree frogs, by hanging a pair of kippers, long past their sell by date, on my mum's washing line. The kippers attracted clouds of flies, the desired effect. But from thereon, I was blamed for every flying insect in the neighbourhood. My neighbour Mrs McCafferty wailed whenever I was in earshot, "If this boy continues with his ways, we'll all be going down with malarials and the bubonics so we will."

I also kept snakes. Non-venomous, but still alarming when they appeared on the doorstep of the non-reptile enthusiast. (Or even worse on the seat of the outside loo.)

At the time I also had a tame Magpie. Unlike her nest companions Maggie had survived when the nest was blown to the ground. Reared entirely on dog food. I don't know if it was the high nutrients present in the diet, or the predisposition for delinquency, coupled with the intelligence tame magpies possess. But by the time she was flying, she was public enemy number one. Chasing cats, stealing clothes pegs and knocking on windows was the lesser of her crimes.

She also had a fascination for spectacles worn by cyclists in motion. And took a dislike to the toupee worn by a local doctor, a keen gardener. One attack took place when the doctor was aboard his ride on mower. Losing control of the machine while being scalped. He found his formerly pristine lawn was now covered in crop circles, while his mass of inanimate black curls ended up in a tree, being fought over by two carrion crows. Maggie's final act of vandalism, was to puncture the silver foil top, of every milk bottle in an unattended milkman's float. The whole street turned out, to inform the milkman who was responsible.

Pointing to my house, where I was quivering behind net curtains, the assembled crowd chanted in unison:

"It's the fly breeder at number 24."

In the early 1960's, my neighbours had a street party, to celebrate the fly breeding, snake charmer's move, from the neighbourhood, to start a career as a zoo keeper. Which I hope you have enjoyed reading about.

Lightning Source UK Ltd.
Milton Keynes UK
UKHW02f0610111018
330371UK00008B/735/P